WISE PUBLICATIONS
part of The Music Sales Group
London / New York / Paris / Sydney / Copenhagen / Berlin / Madrid / Hong Kong / Tokyo

1960 1961 1962 1963 1964 1965 1966 1967 1968 1969

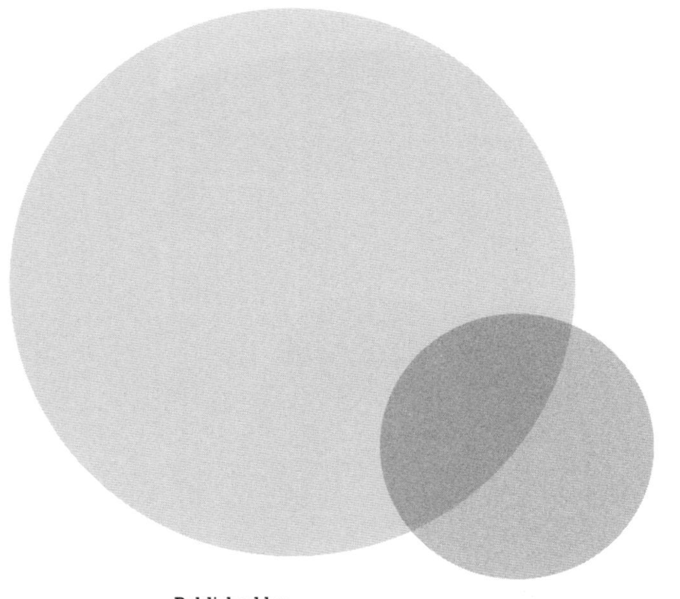

Published by
Wise Publications
14-15 Berners Street, London W1T 3LJ, UK.

Exclusive Distributors:
Music Sales Limited
Distribution Centre, Newmarket Road,
Bury St Edmunds, Suffolk IP33 3YB, UK.
Music Sales Pty Limited
20 Resolution Drive, Caringbah,
NSW 2229, Australia.

Order No. AM991419
ISBN: 978-1-84772-211-9

Compiled by Nick Crispin
Cover design by Fresh Lemon
All photographs courtesy of LFI
Printed in the EU

1980 1981 1982 1983 1984 1985 1986 1987 1988 1989

50 YEARS OF SOUL

Ray Charles

The main building blocks of soul were assembled in the mid-1950s when two major artists, **Ray Charles** and **Sam Cooke**, natural pioneers who instinctively experimented with styles of black American music, independently of each other began mixing strands of blues, rhythm & blues and gospel – chords, song structures, vocal mannerisms – such that the new genre soon termed 'soul' evolved. Better than almost any song imaginable from the period, Brother Ray's 'What'd I Say Part 1' exemplifies this coming together. The call-and-response between Charles' lead and the Raeletts' backing vocals is pure church, but the earthy lyrics are the stuff of gritty rhythm & blues. It was no coincidence that Charles was recording for Atlantic, the seminal New York independent label that remained at the forefront of soul decades after the style's inception.

In the very earliest years of soul's development, the exuberance and drive of early rock'n'roll also had a significant role to play. Take, for example, the versatile **Jackie Wilson**. A dynamic live performer and a superb balladeer, Wilson's repertoire ranged from the slight but infectious 'Reet Petite' (co-written by **Berry Gordy**, later to found Motown) to the towering ballad 'To Be Loved' (another Gordy co-composition), but 'Doggin' Around' had its roots sunk much deeper in the blues.

Gospel's fundamental role in the shaping of soul is nowhere better illustrated than in **Ben E. King**'s 'Stand By Me'. It is, simply, a secular rewrite of the gospel standard 'Lord, Stand By Me', and many of the great soul songs of the '60s have their beginnings in the music sung by the artists and writers in church. It is very rare to find a great soul singer who did not learn their trade by singing in church. (Conversely, it is just as rare to find a young singer today schooled in or influenced first-hand by gospel music; hence soul music in the 1990s and into the new millennium has become something entirely different, a blander pop-attuned vocal style aimed at either fans of bravura ballads or dance music.) Forty-five years ago, however, artists such as **Otis Redding** and **James Brown**, as well as being outstanding rampaging soul men, could slow it way down and emote with great passion and conviction. Otis's tender and pleading 'These Arms Of Mine' is textbook Southern soul balladeering, while the Godfather of Soul's 'Prisoner Of Love' is an even rawer experience as James falls to his knees and pleads. Brown, of course, was a complete originator. Listen to his 'Cold Sweat' in the context of other soul (or any) music of 1967 to get some idea of how fundamentally different his direction and creativity was to anyone else at the time. Both men also recorded for independent labels – Brown at Syd Nathan's King in Cincinatti; Redding for Stax in Memphis – and the mushrooming of small

James Brown

Ben E. King

regional labels which made music that spread nationally, and then internationally, was also so central to the growth of a widely divergent soul music. At this time, the major record labels had no feel for or, indeed, a great interest in the music and largely disregarded the genre.

In fact, Stax's pre-eminence as a fine producer of Southern soul persuaded the New York-based Atlantic Records to send many of their best acts to work first at Stax and later to Muscle Shoals in Alabama. But some singers could just transcend geography and sing Southern in the north. Step forward the incomparable **Solomon Burke**, whose interpretation of **Bert Berns**' 'Cry To Me', was pure get-down Southern balladeering recorded in downtown New York. Burke would soon start recording in the South, but Atlantic wasted absolutely no time at all in sending **Wilson Pickett** down there. They were immediately repaid by the iconic 'In The Midnight Hour', a song **Booker T & The MG**'s guitarist Steve Cropper worked up for Pickett by focusing on the title's phrase which the singer had often used in improvised vocal passages when singing with an earlier group, **The Falcons** out of Detroit. Inevitably, the 'midnight hour' phrase came from gospel. **Eddie Floyd** came from the South but was also in The **Falcons** and he recorded the equally iconic 'Knock On Wood', another Cropper song, at about the same time as Pickett's hit. But the latter's success meant Eddie had to wait for his moment because the label feared one song would swamp the other. Anyone wanting to play soul with a genuine feel for and understanding of the music, really should get all of the above down pat, with a side order of **Booker T & The MG**'s 'Green Onions' for groove. To ignore them is like trying to read or write without learning the alphabet or how to spell the basic vocabulary. One essential is still missing.

Eddie Floyd

Berry Gordy's songwriting experiences for **Jackie Wilson** had taught him the importance of strong material, but later lessons convinced him of the need for a more total control over his work. So he set up Motown. That label's distinctive sound, created in the basement of a small unprepossessing house in Detroit, has become an international template for outstanding and enduring soul music. That his label attracted so many great artists – **Marvin Gaye**, **Stevie Wonder**, **The Miracles**, **The Temptations**, **The Supremes**, **Martha & The Vandellas**, among many others – remains an astonishing achievement. Add to that the armoury of incredible songwriters and producers – **Smokey Robinson**, **Holland-Dozier-Holland**, **Norman Whitfield**, again, among many – and the attainment is magnified a hundredfold. Motown of the '60s is here represented by another of its very best acts, the **Four Tops**, whose cover of **Left Banke**'s 'Walk Away Renee' was another fine vehicle for their bravura baritone lead singer **Levi Stubbs**. And Motown has not been just a '60s fossil in the museum of soul sounds: in the '70s **Marvin Gaye**'s expansive *What's Going On* album, from which 'Inner City Blues (Make Me Wanna Holler)' is taken, exemplified the socio-political path numerous artists took as they grew beyond the broad love-and-good-times/pain-and-heartbreak remit of the mid-'60s.

The Four Tops

By the end the '70s, the global mood had changed again and some artists found it easier to adapt to disco than others. **Diana Ross** found a Chic fit with her **Nile Rodgers**/**Bernard Edwards** written/

produced disco classic 'Upside Down', while the **Commodores**' 'Nightshift', coming in the wake of lead singer **Lionel Richie**'s departure, was a strong reminder that their group was more than just one man. Generations on, **Boyz II Men**'s 1992 Motown hit 'End Of The Road' was a prime example of new jack swing, as that particular offshoot of soul had been rebranded.

It was a constant source of amazement to many of the African-Americans singers of the late '50s and early '60s that the soul music they wrote and sang struck such a resounding chord with folks who lived half a world away in societies linked to theirs by language alone, and sometimes not even that. But from **The Beatles** and **The Rolling Stones** down, the music of Motown, Stax, Atlantic and **James Brown** was pivotal to their growth as musicians and songwriters. Not only are their early albums generously sprinkled with cover versions of blues, R&B and soul standards, their early compositions bear the stamp of careful listening to those styles, and of lessons learned. One of the best British singers to embrace soul interpretations was **Dusty Springfield**, and her 'Son Of A Preacher Man', produced in the USA by Atlantic's **Jerry Wexler**, is a convincing soul performance, regardless of race. Moreover, the simple fact is that many of the great Southern soul songs were written or produced by white Americans or used white Southern musicians who felt and understood the music completely. Dusty had a difficult time recording in the USA with Wexler, mostly because he had recorded with the Queen of Soul herself. Thus **Aretha Franklin** is represented here by her version of 'Don't Play That Song (You Lied)', first recorded by **Ben E. King**, co-written by Atlantic founder **Ahmet Ertegun**, produced by **Jerry Wexler** and recorded with the **Dixie Flyers** down in Miami, Florida.

Dusty Springfield

Musical influences did not always flow only in one direction. Rock had begun to influence soul in the mid-'60s when Motown and Stax artists covered songs by **The Beatles** and **Rolling Stones** and by the end of the decade a multi-racial band of men and women became emblematic of the changing times. **Sly & The Family Stone**'s 'Hot Fun In The Summertime' is a lightly funky appealing pop-soul-rock hybrid that would signal a way forward for anyone eager to make a cross-pollination of styles.

By the mid-'60s, the ability of Atlantic, Stax and, particularly, **Berry Gordy**'s Motown Sound to persistently break into the pop charts on both sides of the ocean raised the stakes for many soul artists and throughout the '70s barriers tumbled and the edges that once defined the soul style gradually began to blur. The singing became a lot less gritty and gruff, the sweetening of strings became more prominent. There were exceptions, naturally, such as **Willie Mitchell**'s productions in Memphis for the Hi label which rekindled Southern soul as illustrated here on **Ann Peebles**' glorious 'I Can't Stand The Rain', while one-off artists such as **Bill Withers** – his 'Lean On Me' was to the '70s what 'Stand By Me' was to the '60s – could create a small but utterly cherishable body of work. However, the general drift of soul music was towards the dancefloor from **George**

Aretha Franklin

McCrae's Miami soul classic 'Rock Your Baby' through the Philly soul of **The Stylistics**' 'Can't Give You Anything (But My Love)' to the Brit-soul of **Billy Ocean**'s 'Love Really Hurts Without You'.

The '70s also saw the emergence of self-contained bands who both sang and played their own instruments, rather than the '50s and '60s soul norm which saw a lead singer backed by a fairly anonymous group of interchangeable backing musicians. **Rose Royce**, mentored by former staff Motown writer/producer **Norman Whitfield**, **Earth, Wind & Fire**, led by one-time **Chess** studio drummer **Maurice White**, Rufus featuring **Chaka Khan** and **Larry Blackmon**'s Cameo were among the best here represented by 'I Wanna Get Next To You', 'September', 'Ain't Nobody' and 'Word Up' respectively.

And in the middle of all that came **Prince**, who for breadth of ability as a bandleader, songwriter and artist harks back to **Ray Charles** and **James Brown**, comparably driven men of another era, each touched by genius at points in their careers.

Alicia Keys

If **Anita Ward**'s 'Ring My Bell' was at the trite end of '70s disco, a couple of years after it **Randy Crawford**'s 'You Might Need Somebody' suggested there would still be a place for the more profound song and performance, the more emotionally committed soul voice. And so it has been, from the pop-savvy of **Michael Jackson**'s light and lilting Human Nature to the big-ballad diva-defining 'Saving All My Love For You' of **Whitney Houston** to **Gnarls Barkley**'s catchy-as-anything 'Crazy' and **Womack & Womack**'s 'Teardrops'. Latterly, the soul genre has widened to redefine itself as an international mass-music with considerably less of that febrile emotional input demanded in the late '50s and early '60s. Also, the people singing have changed. Their experiences are obviously not the same as someone born in the years after the Second World War.

Since the mid-'80s, in the USA male artists have increasingly gravitated towards hip hop and rap where the quality of singing is of no importance whatsoever, although the accompanying beats are invariably lifted off funk and soul records. An honourable exception is **The Roots**, whose **?uestlove** is the conscience tapping into older soul.

This has left the field open to an emergent scene of women singers of varying ability – some very good indeed, some very marketable – starting with the **Jam & Lewis** productions for **Janet Jackson**, and continuing with the soul-pop of **TLC**'s lovely 'Waterfalls', the jazzier shades of **Macy Gray** and **Erykah Badu**, the harder edges of **Mary J. Blige** or the varied ballads/dance appeal of **Toni Braxton**, **Kelis**, **Destiny's Child**, from whence sprang superstar **Beyoncé**, and **Alicia Keys**.

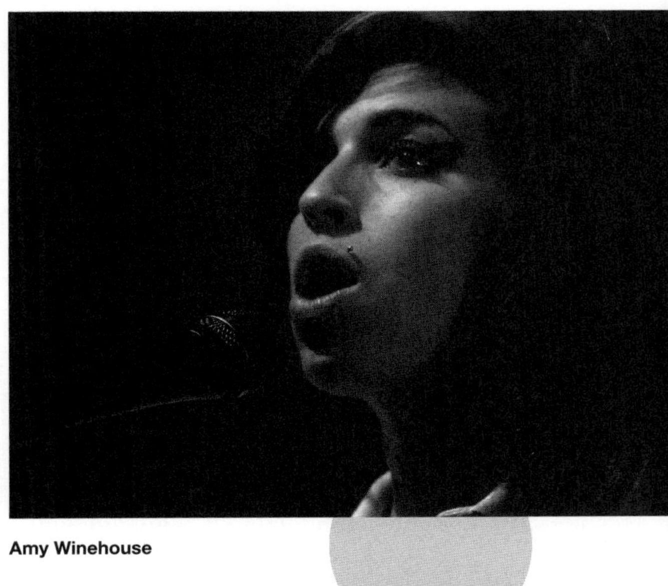

Amy Winehouse

Meanwhile, many young British singers, writers and musicians continued to tap into and forge a very distinct UK 'post-soul' sound, from London's **Soul II Soul** and Bristol's **Massive Attack** to **Portishead** and on to the latest generation who sound as though they have studied their parents' record collections very well indeed: **Joss Stone**, **Duffy**, X Factor-winner **Leona Lewis** and, best of the bunch, **Amy Winehouse** are all represented here.

Geoff Brown

RAY CHARLES

What'd I Say (Part 1)

Words & Music by Ray Charles

A7
E7
B7
A7
E7
B7
N.C.
A7
E7
B7

A7
E7
B7
E7
1. Hey, Ma-ma don't you treat me wrong.
2. See the girl with the dia - mond ring,
3. Tell your Ma-ma, tell your Pa,
Come and love your Dad-dy
she knows how to
I'm gon - na send you back to
A7
E7
all night long, all night long.
shake that thing, al - right now.
Ar - kan - sas. Oh, yes, ma'am.
Hey, hey!
Hey, hey!
You don't do right,
B7
A7
Al - right.
Hey, hey!
don't do right.
3

1, 2.
3.
E7
B7
B7
N.C.
A7
E7
B7
A7
E7
B7
3

E7
4. When you see me in mis - er - y, come on, ba - by,
5. See the girl with the red dress on, she can do the Bird -
A7
E7
see a - bout me now. Hey, hey.
-land all night long. What'd I say?
B7
A7
1.
E7
Al - right.
Al - right.
3
B7
2.
E7
B7
Well, tell me, what'd I say?

E7
Yeah.
Tell me, what'd I say right now?
Ba - by, I wan - na know right now.
A7
Tell me, what'd I say?
And I wan - na know.
Tell me, what'd I say
Ba - by, I wan - na know
E7
right now?
right now.
B7
Tell me, what'd I say?
And I wan - na know.
A7
E7
1.
2.
Tell me, what'd I say? Yeah.
Said, I wan - na know. Yeah.
And I wan - na know,

JACKIE WILSON

Doggin' Around

Words & Music by Lena Agree

B♭
B♭7
down.
'Cause I
E♭
6fr
Edim7
3
can't take it much long - er.
B♭/F
B♭7
My heart's getting weak, it's not get-ting an-y strong - er.
E♭
6fr
Edim7
You keep me so up - set, my head's in a whirl.

C7
F
Cm7
Dm/A
F7
But if you wan-na be my girl you'd bet-ter stop,
8va
Bb
Gm
C7
F7
yeah, dog - - - gin' me a-
3
Bb
Gm
C7
F7
- round.
'Cause if you don't
Bb
Gm
C7
F7
To Coda
stop, ah, I'm gon-na put you
4

B♭
B♭7
down.
Now you
E♭
6fr
Edim7
4
know you, you go out nights
to have your-self a ball.
B♭/F
B♭7
Some-times you don't,
you don't make it home at all.

E♭
6fr
Edim7
I don't mind you hav-in' your-self a real good time,
D.S. al Coda
C7
3fr
F
Cm7
3fr
Dm/A
F7
4
but not what you're try-in' to do, try-in' to make me lose my mind. You'd bet-ter stop
8va
Coda
B♭
Gm
3fr
C7
3fr
F7
Repeat ad lib. and fade
down. Yes, put you

BEN E. KING

Stand By Me

Words & Music by Ben E. King, Jerry Leiber & Mike Stoller

A
see.
sea.
No, I won't be a - fraid; no, I
I won't cry, I won't cry; no, I won't
F♯m E F♯m D E
won't be a - fraid, just as long as you stand, stand by
shed a tear, just as long as you stand, stand by
A A
me. So dar - lin', dar - lin',
me. And dar - lin', dar - lin',
* Dar - lin', dar - lin',
stand by me. Oh, stand
mf
F♯m E F♯m D E
by me. Oh, stand, stand by me,

1, 2.
3.
A
stand by me.
2. If the sky
stand by me. When-
A
-ev - er you're in trou - ble, won't you
stand by me.
Oh, stand
F♯m
E
F♯m
D
by me.
Won't you stand now?
Oh, stand,
E
A
Vocal ad lib, repeat and fade
stand by me,
stand by me.

OTIS REDDING

These Arms Of Mine

Words & Music by Otis Redding

B♭
B♭aug
B♭6
B♭7
E♭
6fr
F7
would let them
hold
you,
oh, how grate - ful
I will be.
These arms of
mine,
they are burn - ing,
burn - ing from want - ing
you.
These arms of
mine,
they are

Ad lib. lyrics for fade:
Come on, come on baby,
Just be my little woman, just be my lover.
I need me somebody, somebody to treat me right,
Oh, I need your arms, lovin' arms to hold me tight.
And I need your tender lips,
To hold me together when I'm around you.

Prisoner Of Love

Words & Music by Leo Robin, Clarence Gaskill & Russ Columbo

♩. = 68
B♭
Cm
3fr
B♭/D
E♭
6fr
Cm7
3fr
F
N.C.
F
N.C.
E
E♭
6fr
F
1. A - lone from night to night you'll find me,
2. From one com - mand I stand and wait now
3. She's in my dreams, a - wake or sleep - ing.
B♭
Dm
G7
too weak to break these chains that bind me.
from one who's mas - ter of my fate now.
Up - on my knees to her I'm creep - ing.

To Coda
Cm
3fr
E♭
6fr
F
E
I need no sha - ckles to re - mind me
I can't es - cape, for it's too late now.
My ver - y life, my life is in her keep - ing.
E♭
6fr
F
E
1.
E♭
6fr
F
E
4
I'm just a pris - 'ner.
Don't let me be a pris - 'ner.
2.
E♭
6fr
F
B♭
F
4
Don't let me be a pris - 'ner.
What's the good of my car - ing,
B♭
F7
B♭
F
if some-one is shar-ing those arms,
but not with me?
Al-

B♭
F
B♭
F7
-though she has an-oth-er and I can't have an-oth-er, for I,
B♭
B♭7
D.S. al Coda
E7
I'm not free.
Coda E♭
6fr
F
E
E♭
4
I'm just a pris - 'ner.
Don't let me be a pris-'ner.
Repeat ad lib. and fade
(Pris-'ner of love)
(Pris-'ner of love)

SOLOMON BURKE

Cry To Me

Words & Music by Bert Russell

E
B
phone, don't you feel like cry - ing?
- fume, don't you feel like cry - ing?
- one, don't you feel like cry - ing?
E
To Coda
Don't you feel like cry - ing? Well, here I am, my
(2°, 3°) Don't you feel like cry - ing? Don't you feel like cry -
B
E
hon - ey: come on, well, cry to me.
- ing? Come on, come on, cry to me.
1.
2.
E7
A
2. When you're all a - Whoa, noth - ing can be

E
sad - der ___ than a glass of wine ___ a - lone.
B
E
Lone - li - ness, lone - li - ness: ___ such a waste of time, ___ oh - ho, yes. ___
E7
A
___ You don't ev - er have to walk a - lone, ___
E
B
___ well, you see. ___ A - come on, ___ take my hand, ___ and

E
N.C.
B
E
N.C.
D.S. al Coda
ba - by, won't you walk with me?
Oh - ho, yeah.
When you're
Coda
B
Don't you feel like a - cry cry cry cry cry cry
E
cry cry cry cry cry cry cry - ing?
Don't you feel like a - cry
B
cry cry cry cry cry
E
cry cry cry cry cry cry cry - ing?

In The Midnight Hour

Words & Music by Wilson Pickett & Steve Cropper

E A E A B A
no-one else_ a-round._____ I'm gon-na take you, girl, and hold__ you, and
B7 A E A E A
do all the things I told__ you in the mid-night hour.__ Yes, I am.__ Oh, yes, I
E A D B E A
am. I'm gon-na wait till the stars come out
E A E A E A E A
and see that twin-kle in your eyes.__ I'm gon-na wait till the mid-night

E A E A E A B
hour, that's when my love be-gins to shine.
You're the on-ly girl I know
A B7 A E A
that real-ly loves me so in the mid-night hour.
Oh,
E A E A D B
yeah, in the mid-night hour.
E A E A E D B

E A E A E A B7
I'm gon-na
E A E A E A E A
wait till the mid-night hour, that's when my love comes tum-bl-ing down. I'm gon-na wait
E A E A E A E A
till the mid-night hour, that's when my love be-gins to shine. Just you and I.
Repeat ad lib. and fade
E A E A E A E A
Oh, ba-by. Just you and I. No-bod-y a-round, ba-by. Just you and I.

Knock On Wood

Words & Music by Steve Cropper & Eddie Floyd

♩ = 104
E
G
A
N.C.
B
D
B
N.C.
A
A6
A
A6
A
1. I don't wan - na lose this good thing
(2.) - sti - tious a - bout you,
(3.) - cret, that wom - an
A6
A
E
E6
E
that I got, 'cause if I do I will
but I can't take no chance. You got me spin -
fills my lov - ing cup; yes, she sees to it

E6 E E6 E E6 E E6
sure - ly, sure - ly lose a lot. (1, 2.) 'Cause your love
- ning, ba - by; ba - by, I'm in a trance.
that I get e - nough. (3.) Just one
A A6 A A6 A A6 A
is bet - ter than an - y love I know.
touch from her, you know it means so much.
E A
It's like thun - der, light - ning;
E A N.C.
To Coda
the way you love me is fright - 'ning. I'd bet - ter knock on wood,
Drums

E
G
A
N.C.
B
D
ba - by.
1.
B
N.C.
2. I'm not su - per -
2.
B
A
G
N.C.
N.C.
N.C.
N.C.
F♯7
G♯7
A7
C7
B7
D.S. al Coda
N.C.
N.C.
3. Ain't no se -
Coda
E
G
A
N.C.
ba - by.
I'd bet - ter

B
D
N.C.
B
N.C.
A
N.C.
G
N.C.
E
knock, knock, knock.
Oh__ yeah,__
A
E
A
__ think I'd bet - ter knock on wood.__
Think I'd bet - ter
E
A
knock on wood.__
Think I'd bet - ter
E
A
Repeat and fade
knock.
Think I'd bet - ter

THE FOUR TOPS

Walk Away Renée

Words & Music by Bob Calilli, Michael Lookofsky & Tony Sansone

♩ = 116
D F♯m/C♯ Bm7 A
A E/G♯ G
1. And when I see the sign that points one
2. From deep in - side the tears I'm forced to
3. Your name and mine in - side a heart on a
Bm/F♯ Bm7♭5/F A/E
way, the lot we used to pass by
cry, from deep in - side the pain
wall, still finds a way to haunt me,

D/F♯
A/E
Bm/D
A/C♯
B7
A
ev - er - y day.
that I chose to hide.
though they are so small.
Just walk a - way
F♯m
D
A
E
Re - née;
you won't see me fol - low you back home.
A
F♯m
D
C♯m
4fr
To Coda
The emp-ty side - walks on my block are not the same;
Now as the rain beats down up - on my wear-y eyes;
The emp-ty side - walks on my block are not the same;

1.
2.
D
A/C♯
Bm7
A
you're not to blame.
for me it cries.
F♯m
Faug
A/E
B/D♯
3
E/D
A/C♯
D
B7
Just walk a - way Re - née; you

D
A
E
A
won't see me fol - low you back home.
Now as the rain
F♯m
D
C♯m
4fr
beats down up - on my wear - y eyes,
D
A/C♯
Bm7
A
D.S. al Coda
for me it cries.
Coda
molto rit.
you're not to blame.

Son Of A Preacher Man

Words & Music by John Hurley & Ronnie Wilkins

♩ = 90
E
E
1. Bil - ly Ray was the preacher's son__ and when his
2. Be - ing good is - n't al - ways eas - y,
A
E
dad-dy would vis - it he'd come__ a - long;
no mat-ter how hard__ I try;
when they gath-ered round and start-ed talk - ing
when he start - ed sweet talk - ing to me,

B
that's when Bil - ly would take me walk - ing,
he'd come and tell me ev - 'ry - thing is al - right,
out through the back yard we'd go walk - ing,
he'd kiss and tell me ev - 'ry - thing is al - right.
1° only
then he'd look in - to my eyes,
Lord knows, to my sur - prise.
Can't I get a - way a - gain to - night?
The
E
A
E
on - ly one who could ev - er reach me was the son of a preach - er man. The

A
E
only boy who could ever teach me
was the son of a preacher man. Yes, he
B
A
was, he was.
Mm, yes, he was.
2° Lord knows, he was.
1.
E
2.
D
How well I re-mem-ber

A
the look that was in his eyes,
steal-ing kiss-es from me on the sly,
B
B♭
B
tak-ing time to make time,
tell-ing me that he's all mine,
E7
learn-ing from each oth-er's know-ing,
look-ing to see how much we've grown and the
A
D
A
on-ly one who could ev-er reach me
was the son of a preach-er man.
The

D
A
on - ly boy_ who could ev - er teach_ me
was the son of a preach - er man. Yes, he
E
D7
was, he was.
Oh, yes, he was.___ The
A
D
A
on - ly one_ who could ev - er (reach / move) me
was the son of a preach - er man. The
Repeat ad lib. and fade
D
A
on - ly boy_ who could ev - er (reach_ / move_) me
was the son of a preach - er man. The

SLY & THE FAMILY STONE

Hot Fun In The Summertime

Words & Music by Sylvester Stewart

♩. = 96
C
Gm(add9)
3fr
C
Gm(add9)
3fr
C
Gm7
3fr
1. End of the spring, and here she comes
2. That's when I had most of my fun
3. First of the fall and then she goes

Dm7♭5
A♭6
Gm7
3fr
B♭7/F
back.
Hi, hi, hi,
back.
High, high, high,
back.
Bye, bye, bye,
E♭
6fr
hi there.
high there.
bye there.
Them
Dm7
G
Dm7/G
G
sum - mer days,
those sum - mer days.
Dm7
Em7
F6
F6/A
1.
G
2, 3.
G
I cloud nine when I

Dm7 Em7 Dm7 G
want to.
Out of school,
Dm7 Em7 Dm7 G
yeah.
Coun-ty fair in the coun-
Dm7 Em7 Dm7 G
-try sun.
And ev-'ry-thing, it's
Dm7 Em7 F6 D7/F♯ G G/G♯ G/A G/E
cool.
Oh, yeah, yeah.

Dm7
Em7
Dm7
G
Hot fun in the sum - mer - time.
Dm7
Em7
Dm7
G
Hot fun in the sum - mer - time.
Dm7
Em7
Dm7
G
Hot fun in the sum - mer - time.
D.S. and fade
Dm7
Em7
F6
D7/F♯
G
G/G♯
G/A
G/B
Hot fun in the sum - mer - time.

Don't Play That Song (You Lied)

Words & Music by Ahmet Ertegun & Benjamin Nelson

Am
F
'cause it brings back mem - o - ries of days that I
he kissed me and he walked a - way. I was on - ly
G7
once knew, the days that I spent with-a you.
sev - en - teen. I nev-er dreamed he'd be so mean. He told me,
1° only
C
Am
Oh no! Don't let him play it. (Oh no!) It fills my
F
heart with pain. Please stop it right a - way,
(It hurts)

G7
'cause I re-mem-ber just-a what it say. It say,
C
Am
("Darl-in', I love you.") ("Darl-in', I
"Darl-in'..." I know that he lied.
"Darl-in'..." Ba-by ba-by you lied.
F
need you.") You know that you lied. ("Darl-in', I love you.") You know that you
You, you lied. You know that you
Gsus4
To Coda
G7
lied, lied, you lied.
lied, (You lied.) lied, (You lied.) lied.

C
(To me.)
Hey, mist - er, don't play it no
Am
more.
Don't play it no more.
F
I can't
G7
D.S. al Coda
stand it! Don't play it no more, (No more.) no more, (No more.) no more.
Coda
G7
Am
G/B
C
(To me.)

Am G/B C Am D7 D11 Dm7/G
C G C
Oh, darl - in', ("Darl - in', I love you.") you know that you lied,
lied.
Am F
yeah.
("Darl - in', I need you.")
You know, I know you lied.
("Darl - in', I
Gsus4 G7
Repeat ad lib. and fade
love you.") Darl - in', you lied, (You lied.) you lied, (You lied.) you lied. Go on, and hurt me. You

James Brown

Ray Charles

Aretha Franklin

Wilson Pickett

MARVIN GAYE

Inner City Blues (Make Me Wanna Holler)

Words & Music by Marvin Gaye & James Nyx

Em7
8va throughout
1. Rock - ets,
(2.)- tion,
moon - shots.
no chance
Spend it on
to in-crease
the have-nots.
fi - nance.
Mon - ey,
Bills pile up
we make
sky
it.
high.
'Fore we see it
Send that boy off
you take it.
to die.
Oh,
A7sus4
A7
make me wan-na holl - er the way they do my life.
Yeah.

1.
2.
A7sus4
A7
Em7
Make me wan-na holl-er, the way they do my life. This ain't liv-in', this ain't liv-in'. No,
no ba-by, this ain't liv-in'. No no no no.
2. In-fla-
life.
Da da da da da, da da da da da da da da da da.
Da da da da da da da da, da da da da da da da da da da. Da da da da da da da da

Em7
Repeat 3 times
da da da_ da da da da da_ da da. 3. Hang ups, let_ downs. Bad_
4. Crime is_ in - creas - ing, trig -
_ breaks, set_ backs. Nat - 'ral fact_
- ger hap - py po - lic - ing. Pan - ic is spread -
_ is oh, hon - ey, that I_ can't pay_ my tax - es. Oh,
- ing. God_ knows where we're head - ing.
A7sus4
A7
make me wan-na holl - er and throw up_ both my hands. Yeah, they
2° vocal ad lib.

A7sus4
A7
make me wan-na holl - er and throw up__ both my hands.
Em7
Da da da da__da da da__ da, da da da__ da da da da da__ da da. Da da da da__da da da__ da,
Dm7
da da da__ da da da da da__ da da.
Vocal ad lib.
1-3.
4.
A♭7
4fr

A7
Free time ad lib.
Dmaj7
Bm
Dmaj7
Moth - er, moth - er ev - 'ry - bod - y thinks we're wrong.
Who are they to judge us simp - ly 'cause we wear our hair long?
a tempo
Gm9
3fr
Repeat ad lib. to fade
Saxophone
Instrumental/Vocal ad lib.

Lean On Me

Words & Music by Bill Withers

Dm Em
Dm/G
C
Dm C7/E F
we all have sor - row;
but, if we are wise,
Em Dm C
Dm C/E G9
C
we know that there's al - ways to - mor - row. Lean on me
C
Dm C7/E F
Em Dm C
Dm Em
(1, 3.) when you're not strong, and I'll be your friend, I'll help you car -
2. Please swal - low your pride if I have faith you need to bor -
Dm/G
C
Dm C7/E F
Em Dm C
- ry on; for it won't be long till I'm gon - na need
- row; for no one can fill those of your needs

Dm C/E G9
1. C
2. C
some - bod - y to lean on.
that you won't let
show.
on.
You just
N.C.
call on me broth - er when you need a hand. We all need some - bod - y to lean on. I just
To Coda
G7 C
D.S. al Coda
might have a prob - lem that you'll un - der - stand. We all need some - bod - y to lean on. 3. Lean on me
Coda
G7 C
C
Dm C7/E F
need some - bod - y to lean on.
4. If there is a load

Em Dm C
Dm Em
Dm/G
C
Dm C7/E F
you have to bear that you can't car - ry, I'm right up the road,
Em Dm C
Dm C/E G9
C
I'll share your load if you just call me.
Dm/C C
(Call me.) ad lib. vocal (Call me.) (Call me.)
1, 2.
3.
(Call me.) (Call me.) (Call me.) (Call me.)

ANN PEEBLES

I Can't Stand The Rain

Words & Music by Ann Peebles, Bernard Miller & Don Bryant

D♭7
A♭7
4fr
how sweet it___ used to be?___
'cause he's not___ here with me.___
G♭
A♭7
When we was to-geth - er___ ev - 'ry-thing_ was so grand._
Whoa, emp-ty pil - low___ where his head___ used to lay.___
C♭7
Now that we've part - ed,___ there's just
I___ know you've got some sweet mem-o-ries, but like the

B♭m7
E♭7
6fr
one sound that I just can't stand. I can't stand the rain
win - dow, you ain't got noth - ing to say. Hey.
1.
A♭7
4fr
a - gainst my win - dow,
D♭7
4fr
A♭7
4fr
bring - in' back sweet mem - o - ries
2. I can't stand the rain
2.
A♭
4fr
G♭

A♭
4fr
C♭7
1. I can't stand the rain
A♭7
4fr
a-gainst my win - dow,
(2.) a-gainst my win - dow,
(3.) get off my win - dow,
D♭7
4fr
A♭7
4fr
Repeat and fade
bring-in' back sweet mem- o - ries.
2. I can't stand the rain
Just keeps on haunt - ing me.
3. Hey, rain
be - cause he's not here with me.

GEORGE McCRAE

Rock Your Baby

Words & Music by Harry Casey & Richard Finch

E♭
6fr
To Coda
take me in your arms,
rock your ba - by.
(On D.S.) Come
Cm
3fr
F
There's noth - in' to it; just say you wan - na do
Yeah, hold me tight with all your
A♭
4fr
it. O - pen up your heart
might, now let your lov - in' flow

B♭
1.
2.
D.S. al Coda
and let the lov - in' start.
real sweet and slow.
Coda
Cm
3fr
on.
F
A♭
4fr
B♭
D.S. and fade

THE STYLISTICS

Can't Give You Anything (But My Love)

Words & Music by Hugo Peretti, Luigi Creatore & George David Weiss

Original key: G minor

Strongly rhythmic ♩ = 114

1. If I had money I'd go wild buy you furs, dress you like a queen, and in a chauffered limousine we'd look so fine.

(2.) promise you the world, can't afford any fancy things, I cannot buy you diamond rings, no string of pearls.

Am G E7 Am F7 E7

Dm
But I'm an or - di - na - ry guy
But my de - vo - tion I will give
E7
and my poc - kets are emp - ty,
all my life just to you girl,
just an
my de -
Dm
E7
G7
or - di - na - ry guy but I'm yours till I die.
-vo - tion I will give for as long as I live.
Dm7
G7
Cmaj7
Am7
I can't give you an - y - thing but my love,

Dm
Dm7/G
C6
but my love.
Dm7
G7
Cmaj7
Am7
I can't give you an - y - thing but my love,
Dm
Dm7/G
1.
C6
E7
but my love.
Am
2.
C6
D.S. to fade
2. I can-not

BILLY OCEAN

Love Really Hurts Without You

Words & Music by Les Charles & Ben Findon

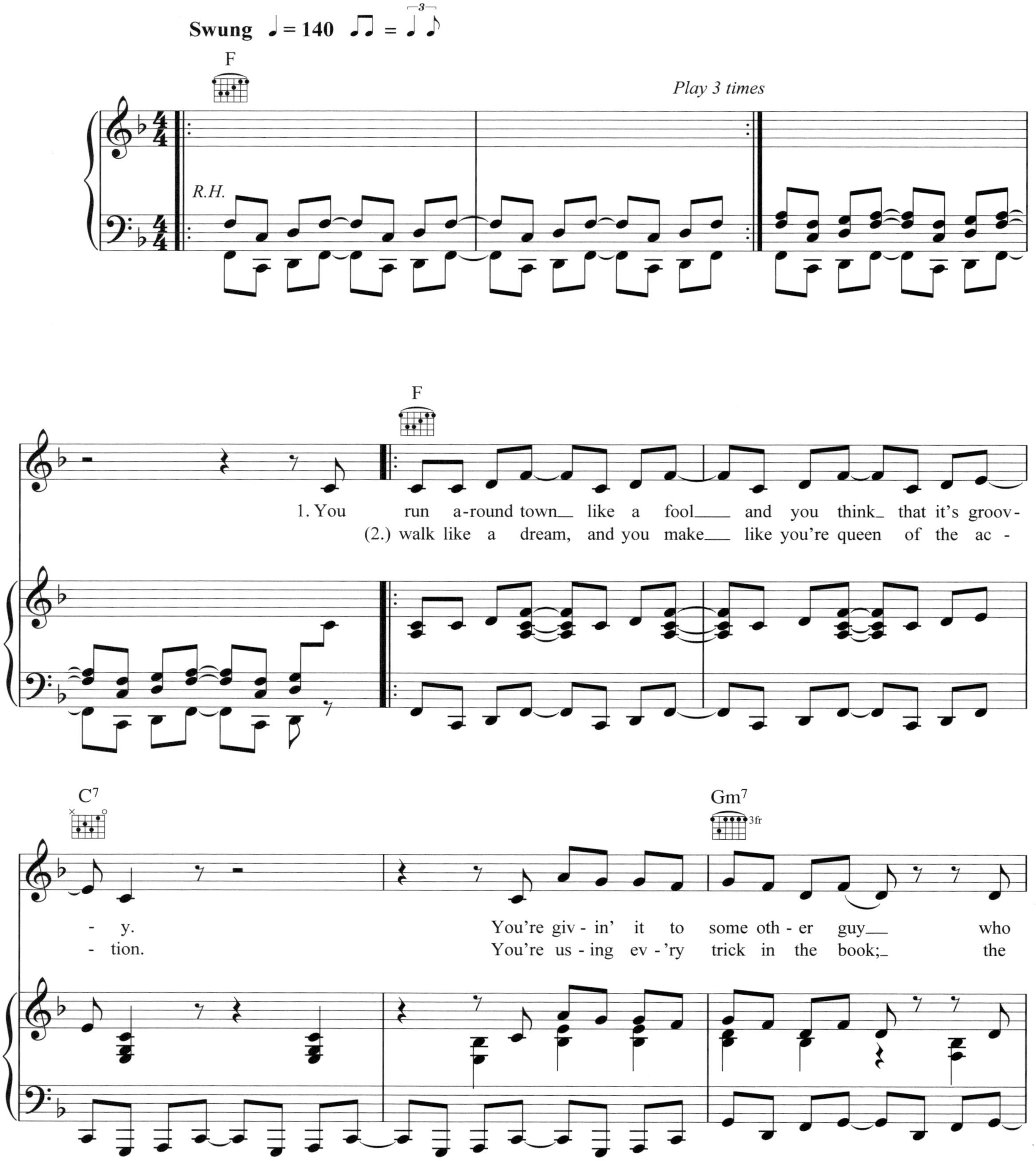

F

1. You run a-round town like a fool and you think that it's groov-
(2.) walk like a dream, and you make like you're queen of the ac-

C7 Gm7 3fr

- y. You're giv - in' it to some oth - er guy who
- tion. You're us - ing ev - 'ry trick in the book; the

Dm
C7
gives you the eye; you don't give noth - in' to me. You
way that you look, you're real - ly some-thing to see. You
F
C7
paint - ed a smile and you dress all the while to ex - cite me,
cheat and you lie to im - press an - y guy that you fanc - y,
Gm7
3fr
but don't you know you're turn - ing me on. I
but don't you know I'm out of my mind, so
B♭
Dm
Csus4
C7
know that it's wrong, but I can't stop this pain in - side me.
give me a sign, and help to ease the pain in - side me.
Ba -

F
C
- by,
love real - ly hurts_ with-out you,
Gm7
3fr
B♭
love real - ly hurts_ with-out you,
and it's break-ing my heart,
but
Dm
C7
F
what can I do?
Ba - by,
love real - ly hurts_ with-out you,
C
Gm7
3fr
love real - ly hurts_through and through,
and it's

B♭
Dm
C7
F
breaking my heart, but what can I do without you?
To Coda
1.
2. You
2.
D.S. al Coda
Coda
G
Ba-
Oh, whoa, ba-
G
D
- by, love really hurts without you,

Am7
C
love real - ly hurts with - out you,
and it's break - ing my heart,
but
Em
D7
G
what can I do?
Ba - by,
love real - ly hurts with - out you,
D
Am7
love real - ly hurts through and through,
and it's
C
Em
D7
Repeat ad lib. and fade
break - ing my heart,
but what can I do with - out you?
Ba -

ROSE ROYCE

I Wanna Get Next To You

Words & Music by Norman Whitfield

wait - in' on you, oh ba -
- by, to see things my way.
But not a
F
F Em Dm Em C
word do you say, you won't e - ven look my way,
yeah.
Girl, I'm

G
spend-ing my dimes, wast-ing my time talk - - in' till I'm
(3.) my mon-ey is low and I know that I can't take you to the
(4.) bend me, shake me, make me. What - ev-er it takes to please you, I'm
F
3
black and blue.
fan - cy plac - es
will-ing to do,
N.C.
Oh can't you see?
you might wan-na go.
'cause you're my dream come true.
1.
F Em Dm
I wan-na get
Em C
next to you.

C
2. Dreams of you and I go sailing by whenever your eyes meet
mine, you're so fine. And girl you make me feel so
F
in - se - cure. You're so beau - ti - ful and pure,

F
Em
Dm
Em
C
why must you be un - kind
and tell me a - bout your kind, blow-in' my
2.
mind? 3. Girl, my,
Still, I wan-na get next to you.
and I wan-na get next to you
I wan - na get next to you.
Fade out 2°
I wan - na get next to you.
Fine
Ba - by, yeah.

F
F
Em
Dm
Em
C
D.S. al Fine
Oh___ yeah._
4. Girl, you can

EARTH, WIND AND FIRE

September

Words by Maurice White & Allee Willis
Music by Al McKay & Maurice White.

F♯m7 Dmaj7 C♯m7 Bm7 C♯7 F♯m7 A13
changing the minds, pretender, while chasing the clouds away.
blue talk and love. Remember how we knew love was here to stay.
Dmaj7 C♯m7 Bm7 C♯m7 F♯m7
Our hearts were ringing in the key, that our souls were sing-
Now December found the love that we shared in Sep-
Dmaj7 C♯m7 Bm7 C♯m7 F♯m7 Dmaj7 C♯m7 Bm7 C♯7
-ing as we danced in the night. Remember how the
-tember. Only blue talk and love. Remember the
F♯m7 A13 B♭11
stars stole the night away? Hey, hey, hey.
true love we share today.

Bm7 E9 C#m7 F#m7 Bm7 E9
Ba de ya, say, do you re-mem-ber? Ba de ya,
C#m7 F#m7 Bm7 E9 C#m7 F#m7
danc-ing in Sep-tem-ber. Ba da ya, nev-er was a cloud-y day.
A13
1.
Dmaj7 C#m7 Bm7 C#m7 F#m7
Ba do da ba do da, ba do da ba do da.
Dmaj7 C#m7 Bm7 C#m7 F#m7 Dmaj7 C#m7 Bm7 C#7
Ba do da ba do da, ba do da ba do da. Ba do da ba do da,

F♯m7
A13
2fr
ba do da.
2. My thoughts are
2.
B♭11
Bm7
E9
C♯m7
4fr
F♯m7
And we say: Ba de ya,
say, do you re-mem-ber?
Bm7
E9
C♯m7
4fr
F♯m7
Bm7
E9
Ba de ya,
danc-ing in Sep-tem-ber.
Ba da ya,
C♯m7
4fr
F♯m7
A13
2fr
Repeat ad lib. to fade
gold-en dreams and shi-ny days.

ANITA WARD

Ring My Bell

Words & Music by Frederick Knight

Fm7
Cm7
3fr
G
now, did you real - ly miss me? I guess
and full of pos - si - bi - li - ties. Well, come on
Cm7
3fr
Fm7
Cm7
3fr
you did, by the look in your eye.
and let your - self be free.
G
Cm7
3fr
Fm7
Well, lay back and re - lax while I
My love for you, so
Cm7
3fr
G
Cm7
3fr
put a - way the dish - es; then you and me
long I've been sav - ing. To - night was made

Fm7
Cm7
3fr
G
can rock - a - bye.
for me and you.
You can ring my
Cm
B♭/C
Fm7
Cm7
bell,
ring my bell.
G
Cm
B♭/C
Fm7
You can ring my
bell,
ring my bell.
Cm7
G
Cm
B♭/C
You can ring my
bell,

Fm7
Cm7
3fr
G
ring my bell.
You can ring my
Cm
B♭/C
Fm7
bell,
ring my bell.
1.
2.
2. The night

Fm7
Cm7
3fr
G
Cm7
3fr
Fm7
Cm7
3fr
(You can ring my bell.) (You can ring my bell.) Ding, dong, ding, ra, ring it.
G
Cm7
3fr
Fm7
You can ring my bell, an - y - time, an - y - where.
Cm7
3fr
1.
G
2.
G
D.S. to fade
Ring it, ring it, ring it, ring it. Ow! ring it.) You can ring my

DIANA ROSS

Upside Down

Words & Music by Bernard Edwards & Nile Rodgers

F♯m7 B7 E F♯m7 B7
Up - side down, boy, you turn me. In - side out and
E F♯m7 B7 E F♯m7
round and round. Up - side down, boy, you turn me.
B7 E F♯m7 G G♯
3fr 4fr
In - side out and round and round. 1, 3. In -
2. I
Am7
-stinc - tive - ly you give to me the love that I need, I
know you got charm and ap - peal, you al - ways play the field. I'm

cher - ish the mo - ments with you. Re - spect - ful - ly, I say to thee, I'm a -
cra - zy to think you are mine. As long as the sun con -
- ware that you're cheat - ing, when no - one makes me feel like you do.
- tin - ues to shine, there's a place in my heart for you, that's the bot - tom line.
1, 2.
3.
Am7
F♯m7
B7
E
F♯m7
Up - side down, boy, you turn me.
B7
E
F♯m7
In - side out and round, round.

B7
E
F♯m7
Up - side down, boy, you turn me.
In - side out and round and round.
Up - side down you're turn - ing me, you're giv - ing love in - stinc - tive - ly.
Round and round you're turn - ing me, I say to thee, re - spect - ful - ly.
Repeat and fade

RANDY CRAWFORD

You Might Need Somebody

Words by Tom Snow & Nan O'Byrne
Music by Tom Snow

D/E
Em7
Am7
G/A
1. When some - bod - y
reach-es for your heart
2° Instrumental ad lib.
Am7
G/A
B
D/E
Em7
o-pen up and let them through.
'Cause ev-'ry - bod - y
Am7
G/A
Am7
G/A
D
needs some-one a-round,
things can tum - ble down on you.
D/E
Em7
Am7
G/A
2. You'll dis - cov - er
when you look a-round,
3. If there's fire
store it in your heart

Am7
G/A
B
you don't have to be a - lone.
and you're sure it's strong and right.
Just one
Keep it
D/E
Em7
Am7
G/A
lov - er
is all you need to know
burn - ing,
through the cold and dark,
Am7
G/A
D
G/B
when you're feel-ing all a-lone.
it can warm your lone-ly nights.
Oh,
Am9
you might need some - bod - y,
you might need some - bod - y too.

Bm7
A
Em7
(You might need some - bod - y too.)
Am9
You might need some - bod - y.
You might need some - bod - y too.
1.
2.
Bm7
A
Em7
Em7
(You might need some-bod-y too.)
need some - bod-y too.)
Am9
You might need some - bod - y,
you might need some - bod - y too.

Bm7
A
Em7
(You might need some - bod - y too.)
Am9
You might need some - bod - y.
You might need some - bod - y too.
Bm7
A
Em7
(You might need some - bod - y too.)
You might
Repeat ad lib. to fade
need some - bod - y too.
(Need some - bod - y.)

Human Nature

Words & Music by Steve Porcaro & John Bettis

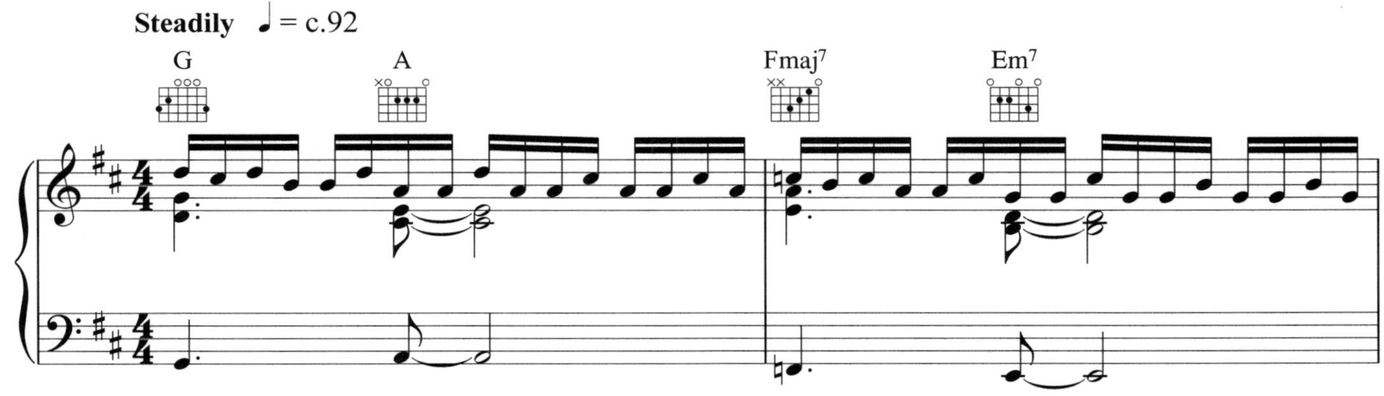

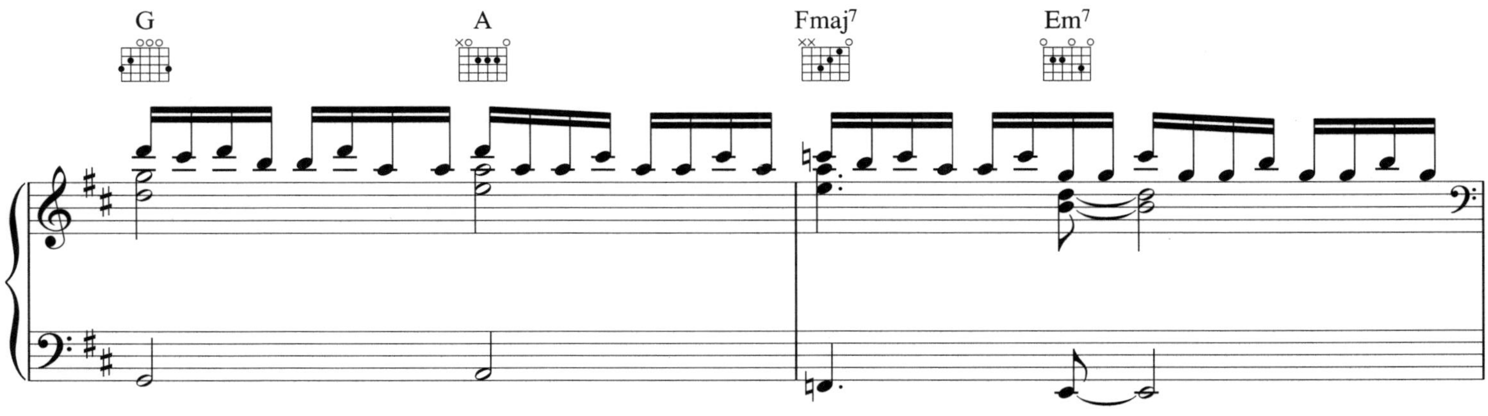

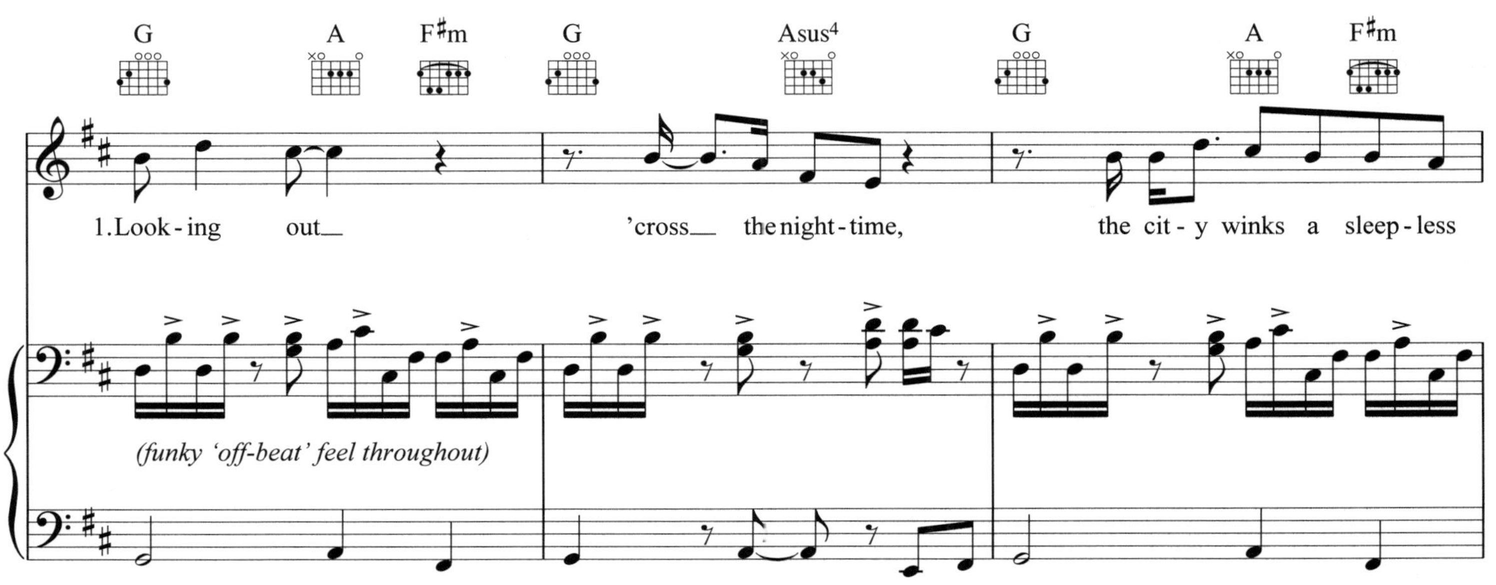

G
Asus4
G
A
F#m
G
Asus4
eye.
Hear her voice
shake my win-dow,
G
F#m7
Em7
Asus4
G
A
F#m
sweet se-du - cing sighs.
1. Get me out
2. Reach-ing out
G
Asus4
G
A
F#m
in - to the night-time,
to touch a strang - er,
four walls won't hold me to -
e - lec - tric eyes are ev - 'ry -

G
Asus4
G
A
F♯m
G
Asus4
-night.
If this town
is just an ap-ple,
-where.
See that girl,
she knows I'm watch-ing,
G
F♯m7
Em7
Asus4
then let me take a bite.
she likes the way I stare.
If they say
G
Asus4
D
D/C♯
D/B
D/A
why, why,
tell 'em that is hu-man na-ture,

G A Em7 Bm
why, why, do they / does he do me that way? If they say
G A D D/C♯ D/B D/A
why, why, tell 'em that is hu - man na - ture,
1. 2.
G A Em7 A11 Em7 Bm7/A
2fr
why, why, do they / does he do me that way? do me that way? I'm like
Em7 Bm7/A Em7 Bm7/A Em9
2fr
2fr
liv-ing this way, I'm like lov-ing this way.

Bm7/A
2fr
G
A
8va
That way,
that way,
Fmaj7
Em7
G
A
(8)
8va
that way,
that way.
Fmaj7
Em7
G
A
F#m
(8)
Look - ing out

G Asus4 G A F#m
a - cross the mor - ning, the cit - y's heart be - gins to
G Asus4 G A F#m G Asus4
beat. Reach - ing out, I touch her shoul - der,
G F#m7 Em7 Asus4
I'm dream - ing of the street. If they say
G A D D/C# D/B D/A
why, why,
tell 'em that is hu - man na - ture,
shall I touch her, ss - ss - ss - ss,

G A Em7 Bm G A
why, why, does he do me that way? If they_ say why, why,
D D/C# D/B D/A G A Em7 A11
oo,_ sev-en, why, why, does he do me that way? If they_ say
G Asus4 D D/C# D/B D/A G A
why, why, oo,_ sev-en, why, why, does he

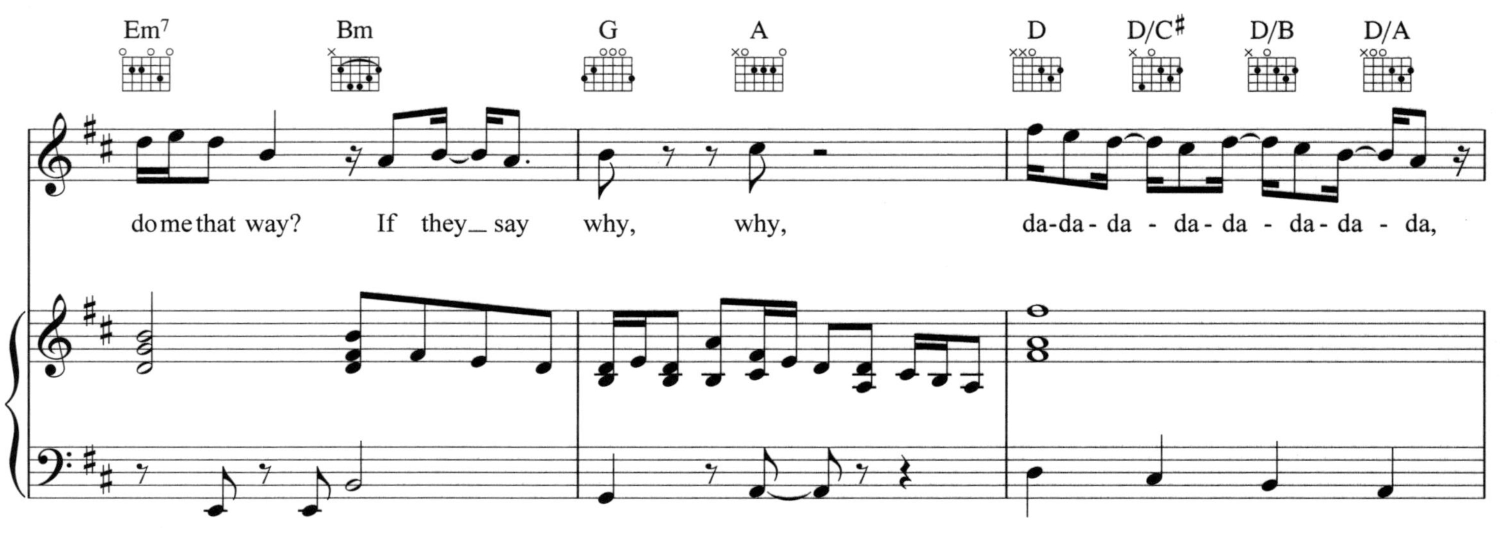
Em7
Bm
G
A
D
D/C♯
D/B
D/A
do me that way? If they say why, why, da-da-da - da-da - da-da - da,

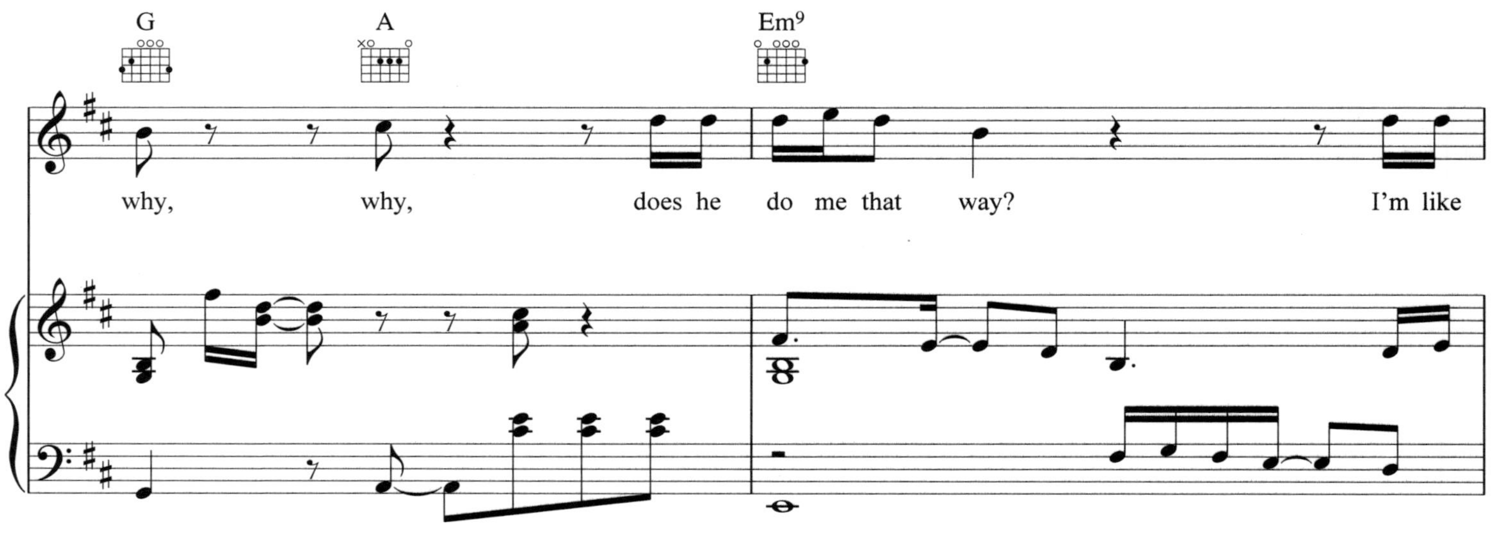
G
A
Em9
why, why, does he do me that way? I'm like

A11
G
A
8va
3
liv-ing this way, wah - oo,

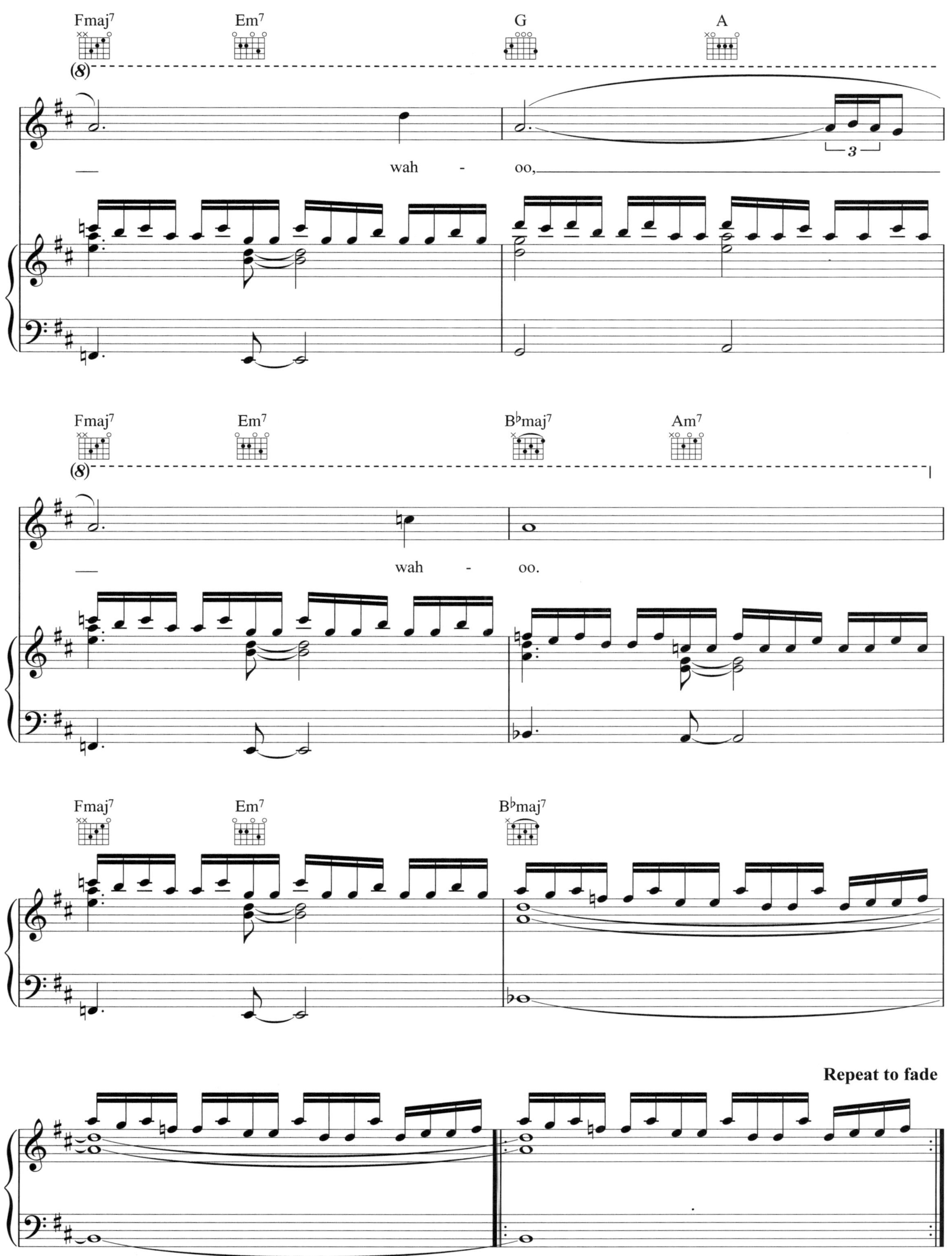
Fmaj7
Em7
G
A
(8)
wah - oo,
3
Fmaj7
Em7
B♭maj7
Am7
(8)
wah - oo.
Fmaj7
Em7
B♭maj7
Repeat to fade

RUFUS & CHAKA KHAN

Ain't Nobody

Words & Music by David Wolinski

Em G N.C. Em G
What was I gon - na do? I let my-self go. And now we fly through the stars
Bm G Em G N.C.
and hope this night will last for - ev - er.
Em G Bm G Em G
I've been wait - ing for you, it's been so long. I knew just what I would do
Bm G Em G
when I heard your song. You filled my heart with a kiss,

Bm G Em G Bm G
you gave me free-dom. You knew I could not re-sist, I need-ed some-one.
N.C.
And now we're fly-ing through the stars and hope this night will last for-ev-er.
Em D Bm7 C
Huh, huh, huh, huh. Ain't no-bod-y, loves me bet-ter,
Em D Bm7 C Em D
makes me hap-py, makes me feel this way. Ain't no-bod-y,

Bm7 C Em D Bm7
loves me bet - ter, ain't no - bod - y, loves me bet - ter than
Em G Bm G Em G Bm G
(you.)
N.C.
I wait for night time to come, to bring you to me. I can't be - lieve I'm the
one, I was so lone - ly. I feel like no - one could feel,

I must be dream-ing.
I want this dream to be real,
I need this feel - ing.
I make my wish up - on a star
and hope this night will last for - ev - er.
Em
D
Bm7
C
I make my wish up - on a star
and hope this night will last for - ev - er.
Huh, huh, huh, huh.

Em
G
Bm
G
Ain't no - bod - y,
loves me bet - ter,
Em
G
Bm
G
makes me hap - py,
makes me feel this way.
Em
G
Bm
G
Em
G
Ain't no - bod - y,
loves me bet - ter,
ain't no - bod - y
Bm
G
Em
D
loves me bet - ter than you.

Bm7
C
Em
D
Spoken: We stare into each other's eyes and what we see is no surprise... (repeat)
Spoken: We've got a feeling most would treasure... (repeat)
And a love so deep we can - not mea - sure.

Em
G
Bm
G
Ain't no - bod - y,
loves me bet - ter,
Em
G
Bm
G
makes me hap - py,
makes me feel this way.
Em
G
Bm
G
Em
G
Ain't no - bod - y.
Bm
G
Em
G
Bm
G
N.C.
Ain't no - bod - y
loves me bet - ter than you.

THE COMMODORES

Nightshift

Words & Music by Dennis Lambert, Francine Golde & Walter Orange

D♭add9
E♭5
sing a song, his heart in ev - 'ry line.
A♭
4fr
Fm7
E♭5
Marv - in, song of the joy and pain, he o - pened
D♭add9
E♭5
up our mind and I still can hear him say.... oh
Fm7
B♭m7
E♭sus4
6fr
talk to me so you can see what's go - ing on.

Fm7
B♭m7
D♭maj7
4fr
Say you will sing your_ songs_ for ev-er more. Gon-na be some
A♭
4fr
Fm
E♭5
sweet sounds_ com-ing down_ on the night-shift. I bet you're
8vb
D♭add9
A♭
4fr
E♭11
sing-ing proud_ oh,_ I bet you pull a crowd._ Gon-na be a
8vb
etc.
A♭
4fr
Fm
E♭5
long night,_ it's gon-na be al - right_ on the night shift.

D♭
4fr
E♭
6fr
You've found an - oth-er home, no I know you're not a - lone on the
A♭
4fr
Fm
D♭
4fr
night- shift. Oh, you've found an - oth-er home, I know you're
E♭
6fr
A♭5
4fr
Fm
E♭sus2
not a-lone on the night shift.
Coda
E♭
6fr
Fm
A♭
4fr
not a - lone on the night-shift. Gon-na be some sweet sounds

Verse 2:
Jackie, hey what you doing now?
It seems like yesterday
When we were working out
Jackie, you set the world on fire
You came and gifted us
Your lovin' lifted us higher and higher
Keep it up and we'll be there at your side
Say you will sing your songs for evermore.

Gonna be some sweet sounds *etc.*

Saving All My Love For You

Words & Music by Gerry Goffin & Michael Masser

F♯m7
B/F♯
F♯m7
B/F♯
try to re - sist, be - ing last on your list, but
each time I try, I just break down and cry, 'cause I'd
A
A/G♯
A/F♯
A/E
G♯m7
4fr
C♯7
4
no oth - er man's gon - na do.
rath - er be home feel - in' blue.
So I'm
Dmaj7
C♯m7
Bm7
1.
Amaj7
F♯m7
sav - ing all my love for you.

2.
Bm7
E7(sus4)
Amaj7
G♯m7
4fr
C♯7
2. It's
You used to tell me we'd
F♯m7
Bm7
E7(sus4)
A
run a-way to-geth-er;
love gives you the right to be free.
You
D♯m7
G♯7
C♯maj7
said:
"Be pa-tient, just wait a lit-tle long-er."
But
F♯m7
B11
E7(sus4)
Amaj7
F♯m7
that's just an old fan-ta-sy.
I've got to get read-y, just a
cresc.
mf

Bm7
E7(sus4)
Amaj7
F#m7
few min - utes more. Gon - na get that old feel - ing when you
Bm7
E7(sus4)
F#m7
B/F#
walk through that door. 'Cause to - night is the night for
F#m7
B/F#
A
A/G#
A/F#
A/E
4
feel - ing all right. We'll be mak - ing love the whole night
4
G#m7
C#7
Dmaj7
C#m7
Bm7
Dmaj7
C#m7
Bm7
4fr
through, so I'm sav - ing all my love, yes I'm sav - ing all my love, yes I'm
f

Dmaj7 C♯m7 Bm7 Amaj7 F♯m7 Bm7 E7(sus4)
sav - ing all my love for you.
Amaj7 F♯m7 Bm7 E7(sus4)
No oth - er wom - an is gon - na love you more. 'Cause to -
mf
f
F♯m7 B/F♯ F♯m7 B/F♯
- night is the night that I'm feel - ing all right. We'll be
ff
A A/G♯ A/F♯ A/E G♯m7 C♯7
4fr
mak - ing love the whole night through; so I'm

Dmaj7 C♯m7 Bm7 Dmaj7 C♯m7 Bm7
sav - ing all my love, yes I'm sav - ing all my lov - ing, yes I'm

Dmaj7 C♯m7 Bm7 Amaj7 F♯m7 Bm7 E7(sus4)
sav - ing all my love for you. For
mf

rall.
Amaj7 F♯m7 Bm7 E7(sus4) A
you.

CAMEO

Word Up

Words & Music by Larry Blackmon & Tomi Jenkins

Gm
3fr
F
E♭
6fr
F
1. Yo, pret - ty la - dies a - round the world, got a weird thing to show you, so tell
(2.) suck - er D. J's who think you're fly. There's got to be a rea - son and we
Vocal ad lib.
G
Gm
3fr
F
all the boys and girls. Tell your broth - er, your sis - ter and your ma - ma too 'cause we're a -
know the rea - son why. You try to put on those airs and act real cool but you
E♭
6fr
F
G
Gm
3fr
- bout to go down and you know just what to do. Wave your hands in the air like
got - ta re - al - ise that you're act - ing like fools. If there's mu - sic we can use it, we're
F
E♭
6fr
F
G
you don't care. Glide by the peo - ple as they start to look and stare. Do your
free to dance. We don't have the time for psy - cho - lo - gi - cal ro - mance. No ro -

Gm
3fr
F
E♭
6fr
F
dance, do your dance, do you dance quick, ma - ma.
-mance, no ro-mance, no ro-mance for me, ma - ma.
Come on ba-by tell me
G
G7
To Coda
F7sus4
F
what's the word. Oh, word up, ev-'ry - bod - y says.
1.
E♭
6fr
F
G
G7
When you hear the call you've got-ta get it un-der way. Word up! It's the
F7sus4
F
E♭
6fr
F
G
code word. No mat-ter where you say it, you know that you'll be heard. 2. Now all you

2.
G
N.C.
get it un-der way. Ow!
Gm
3fr
Oh.
3
Dial L for love.
G7
F7sus4
F
E♭
6fr
F
Vocal ad lib.

G
G7
F7sus4
F
E♭
6fr
F
Just
G
Gm
3fr
come on all you peo-ple sing…
Dou-ble-U O R D up.
Dou-ble-U O R D up.
Dou-ble-U O R D up.
D.S. al Coda
N.C.
Repeat ad lib.
Dou-ble-U O R D up.
Coda
G
Repeat ad lib. to fade
Oh!

Adore

Words & Music by Prince

Gadd9
C
G/B
Un - til the end of time, I'll be there for you. You own my
2° only (That's why)
Am7
D11
Gadd9
heart and mind; I tru - ly a - dore you. If God one day
C
G/B
Am7
D11
struck me blind, you're beau - ty I'd still see. Love's too weak to de - fine just what you mean to me.
G
C
3
1. From the first mo - ment I saw you, ooh, I knew you were the one.
2. When we be mak - ing love, I on - ly hear the sounds

G/B
Am7
D11
That night I had to call you. I was rap-ping till the sun came
of heav-en-ly an-gels cry-ing up a-bove; tears of joy pour-ing down
1.
G
C
G/B
up, tell-ing you just how fine you look; in a word, you were sex. All of my
Am7
D11
G
C
cool at-ti-tude you took. My bod-y was next: you made love to me like you were a-fraid.
G/B
Am7
D11
A♭
4fr
Was you a-friad of me? Was I the first? Was I your ev-'ry fan-ta-sy?
3
3

2.
G
F
C
on us. They know we need each oth - er; they know you are my fix.
I know that you know I ain't cheat-ing ba-by. They know this is se-ri-ous, I ain't funk-ing just for
kicks. No, this con-di-tion I've got is cru-cial, cru-cial, ba-by.
C7
You could say that I'm a ter-mi-nal case; you could burn up my clothes, smash up my ride,

G
F
C
3
3
3
but I got to have your face all up in the place. I'd like to think that I'm a man of ex-qui-site taste:
G
F
C
6
3
3
hun-dred per-cent I-ta-li-an silk, im-port-ed E-gyp-tian lace. Noth-ing, ba-by, I said noth-ing, ba - by could com-pare
G
F
C7
3
3
to your love - ly face. Do you know what I'm say-ing to you this eve-ning? Try'n', try'n' to
A7
D7
N.C.
say, just try'n' to say that, un - til the end of time, I'll be there

G
Em
G/D
for you,
be there for you.
You own my
C
D
G
Em
heart, own my mind.
I tru - ly adore you.
G/D
C
D
3
Ooh,
you don't know what you mean to me.
Gadd9
C
G/B
(Un - til the end of time, I'll be there for you.
You own my
Ad lib. vocal overlay

Am7
D11
Gadd9
C
heart and soul; I tru - ly a - dore you, a -
G/B
Am7
D11
Gadd9
- dore you.)
(Un - til the
Ad lib. vocal overlay continues
C
G/B
Am7
D11
end of time, I'll be there for you. You own my heart and mind; I tru - ly a - dore you.
Gadd9
C
G/B
If God one day struck me blind, you're beau - ty I'd still see. Love's too weak

1.
2.
Am7
D11
to de - fine just what you mean to me.)
to de - fine just what you mean to me.)
Gadd9
C
G/B
(Un - til the end of time.)
(Un - til the
Ad lib. vocal overlay continues
Am7
D11
G
end of time.)
end of time.)
(Girls) Ah, ah, ah, ah,
poco rit.
D7
G6
ah, ah, ah, ah, ah, ah, ah, ah, ah.

WOMACK & WOMACK

Teardrops

Words & Music by Zekkariyas & Zeriiya Zekkariyas

F
Dm7
G
Am
(1.) and cry, The next time I'll be true,
(2.) - cin' 'round, re - minds me, ba - by, of you.
F
Dm7
yeah. Fe - ver for lost ro - mance re -
I real - ly let you down. The
(3.) in - side, she
G
Am
F
Dm7
- mind me ba - by of you. I took a cra - zy chance. The
next time I'll be true, yeah. I took a cra - zy chance. She
cries on ev - er - y tune I break - ing down and cry. She

G
Am
G Am
G Am
N.C.
next time, I'll be true, I'll be true, I'll be true.
cries on ev-er-y tune, ev-'ry tune, ev-'ry tune.
cries on ev-er-y tune, ev-'ry tune, ev-'ry tune.
F
Dm7
G
Am
Foot-steps on the dance floor re-mind me, ba-by, of you.
F
Dm7
Tear-drops in my eyes,
G
Am
F
Dm7
next time I'll be true, yeah. Whis-pers in the pow-

G
Am
G Am
-der room. She cries on ev-er-y tune, ev-'ry tune,
G Am
G
Am
Em7
ev-'ry tune. And the mu - sic don't feel
Dm7
G
like it did when I felt it with you. Noth-ing that
Am
Em7
Dm7
To Coda
I do or feel ev-er feels like I felt it with you.

G
Em7
F
Dm7
G
Am
F
Dm7
G
Am
D.S. al Coda
2. When I'm dan -
3. Hurt - ing deep
Coda
Am
Em7
No, no. And the mu - sic don't feel like it did when I

Dm7
G
Am
Em7
felt it with you.
Noth-ing that I do or feel
ever feels like I felt it with you.
Oh, oh.
Oh, oh.
Oh, oh.
Oh, oh, oh.
F
Dm7
G
Am

F
Dm7
G
Am
Fe-ver for lost ro-mance.
-zy chance.
1.
2.
I took a cra-
Lov-ers hold - ing hands
re-mind me, ba-by, of you.
Repeat w/vocal ad lib. to fade

Billy Ocean

Womak & Womak

Chaka Khan

Prince

Erykah Badu

SOUL II SOUL

Back To Life (However Do You Want Me)

Words & Music by Beresford Romeo, Caron Wheeler, Simon Law & Paul Hooper

Fm7
Dm7
Dm9
be there_ for you.
How - ev - er do you
cont. sim.
Am9sus4
Dm7
Dm9
want_ me?
How - ev - er do you
need_ me? (How?)
How - ev - er do you
Am9sus4
Dm7
Dm9
want_ me?
How - ev - er do you
need_ me?
How - ev - er do you
Am9sus4
Dm7
Dm9
want_ me?
How - ev - er do you
need_ me?
How - ev - er do you

Am9sus4
Dm7
N.C.
want_ me? How - ev - er do you need_ me?
N.C.
Back to life,
back to the pre - sent time.
Back from a fan - ta -
- sy, yes.
Tell me now,
take the in - i - tia - tive. I'll

Em7
leave it in your hands___ un - til you're read - y.___
Dm7
Dm9
Am9sus4
___ How - ev - er do you want_ me? How - ev - er do you
Dm7
Dm9
Am9sus4
need_ me? (How?) How - ev - er do you want_ me? How - ev - er do you
Dm7
Dm9
Am9sus4
need_ me? How - ev - er do you want_ me? How - ev - er do you

Dm7
Dm9
Am9sus4
need_ me? How - ev - er do you want_ me? How - ev - er do you
Dm7
N.C.
Am9sus4
need_ me? How-ev - er do you
Dm7
Dm9
Am9sus4
Dm7
N.C.
need_me? How-ev-er do you need_me?
I live at_ the top of the block._ No more_ room_ for
Drums

trou - ble and fuss.
Need a change, a
pos - i - tive change.
Look, look, it's me writ-ing on the
wall.
How-ev-er do you
Dm9
Am7
want me? How-ev-er do you need me? (How?) How - ev - er do you

1.
Dm9
Am7
want_ me? How-ev-er do you need_ me? How-ev-er do you
2.
Am7
Am9sus4
need_ me?
Dm7
Am9sus4
Dm7
N.C.
Back to life, back to the day we had. Let's end this fool - ish

game.
Hear me out,
don't let it waste a-way.
Make up your mind so I know where I stand.
How-ev-er do you
N.C.
want me?
How-ev-er do you need me? (How?)
How - ev - er do you
want me?
How-ev-er do you need me?
Repeat ad lib. to fade
How-ev-er do you

LIVING COLOUR

Love Rears Its Ugly Head

Words & Music by Vernon Reid

C7
B♭7
F7
3fr
ooh.
Du du du du du du du du du du du du
C7
B♭7
F7
A♭
4fr
du du du du du du du du.
C7
B♭7
F7
1. I al - ways thought that our re - la - tion - ship was cool.
2. And when I come home late you don't com - plain or call.
3. I'm stand - ing at the al - tar as they play the Wed - ding March.
C7
B♭7
F7
You played the role of hav - ing sense, I al - ways played the fool.
So as a con - se - quence I don't go out at all.
I'm in a black tux - edo with my col - lar full of starch.

C7
Bb7
F7
Now something's dif-f'rent, I don't know the rea-son why.
My friends are fright-ened, they don't know what's go-ing on.
She looks as love-ly as she's ev-er gon-na get.
C7
Bb7
F7
N.C.
To Coda
When ev-er we se-pa-rate I al-most wan-na cry.
They think you put a spell on me and now my mind has gone.
I wake up from this night-mare in a pool of sweat.
Eb5
Dm7
C7
Bb7
Oh no, please not that a-gain.
F7
N.C.
Eb5
Dm7
Love rears it's, it's ug-ly head.

1.
C7
B♭7
F7
C7
B♭7
F7
2.
C7
B♭7
F7
Guitar/Vocal ad lib.
C7
B♭7
F7
N.C.
A♭
Gm
Fsus2
Love's
C
B♭/D
E♭
not so bad they say.
But you nev - er know where

C♯
4fr
C7
3fr
B♭7
F7
love is gon - na go.
Does an-y-bod-y
C7
3fr
B♭7
F7
D.S. al Coda
real - ly know?
(Spoken) Check this out...
Coda
E♭5
6fr
Dm7
C5
3fr
B♭5
6fr
Oh no, no, no, no, not that a-gain.
F
N.C.
E♭
6fr
Dm7
Yeah, yeah, yeah, yeah, yeah. I'm not go - ing, oh, I'm not go - ing when

C5
Bb5
F
N.C.
Eb5
3fr
6fr
love rears up it's ug - ly head.
No, not me not.
Dm7
C5
Bb5
F
N.C.
No, no, not me. When love rears up it's, love rears up it's, ug-ly, ug - ly, ug - ly. ug-ly head.
Eb5
6fr
Dm7
N.C.
What ya gon-na do Lord, what ya gon-na do when it comes and gets
C7
Bb7
F7
C7
Bb7
N.C.
you?
Oh!

Unfinished Sympathy

Words & Music by Robert Del Naja, Grantley Marshall, Andrew Vowles, Shara Nelson & Jonathan Sharp

Gm7
3fr
C
1. I know that I've_ i - ma - gined love_ be - fore_
2. The cur - ious - ness_ of your_ po - ten - tial kiss_
Gm7
3fr
C
and how_ it could_ be with_ you.
has got_ my mind and bod - y ach - ing.
Am
Real - ly hurt_ me, ba - by, real - ly hurt_ me, ba - by.
Real - ly hurt_ me, ba - by, real - ly hurt_ me, ba - by.
Dm
How can you have_ a day_ with - out_ a night?_
How can you have_ a day_ with - out_ a night?_

Gm6/B♭
You're the book that I have o - pened,
You're the book that I have o - pened,
and now I've got to know much more.
and now I've got to know much more.
Gm6/A
Dm7
F
G(sus2)
Dm7
F
G(sus2)

Gm7
3fr
C
Like a soul with-out a mind
in a bod-y with-out a heart
Gm7/B♭
Gm6/A
I'm miss-ing ev - 'ry part.
Hey,
hey,
hey,
ay,
ay.
Dm7
F
G(sus2)
Dm7

F
G(sus2)
Gm7
3fr
C
Gm7/B♭
G6/A
Ay, ay, ay, ay.
Dm7
Ay. Like a soul with - out a mind in a bod - y with - out a heart
F
G(sus2)
Play 11 times
I'm miss - ing ev - 'ry part.

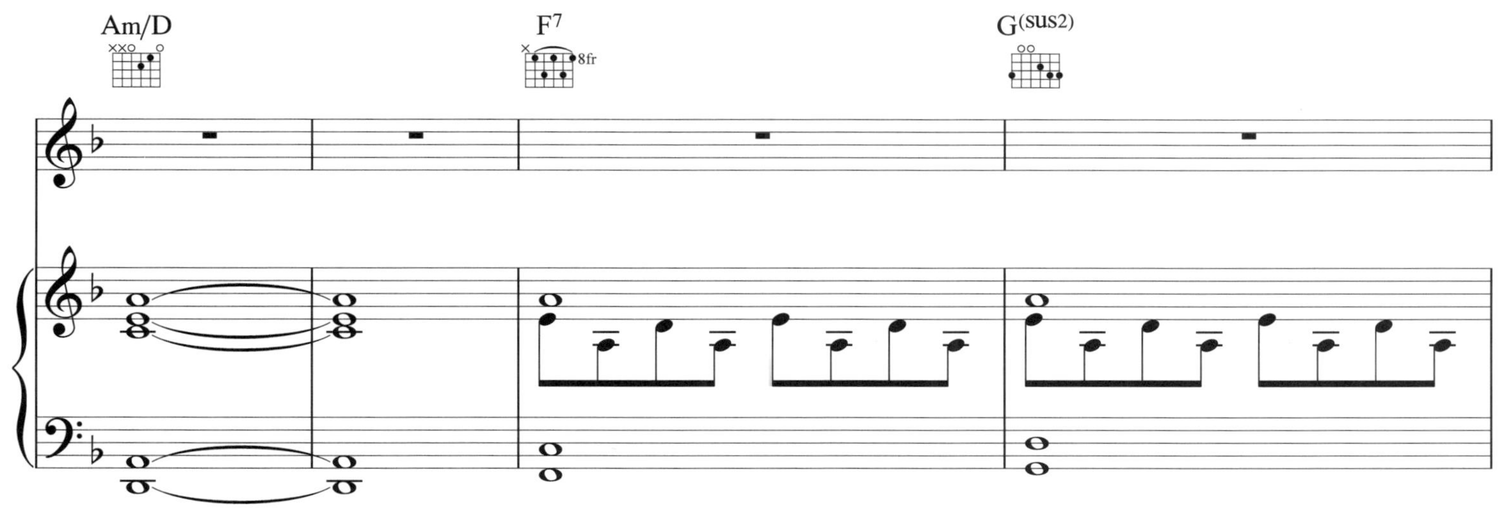
Am/D
F7
8fr
G(sus2)

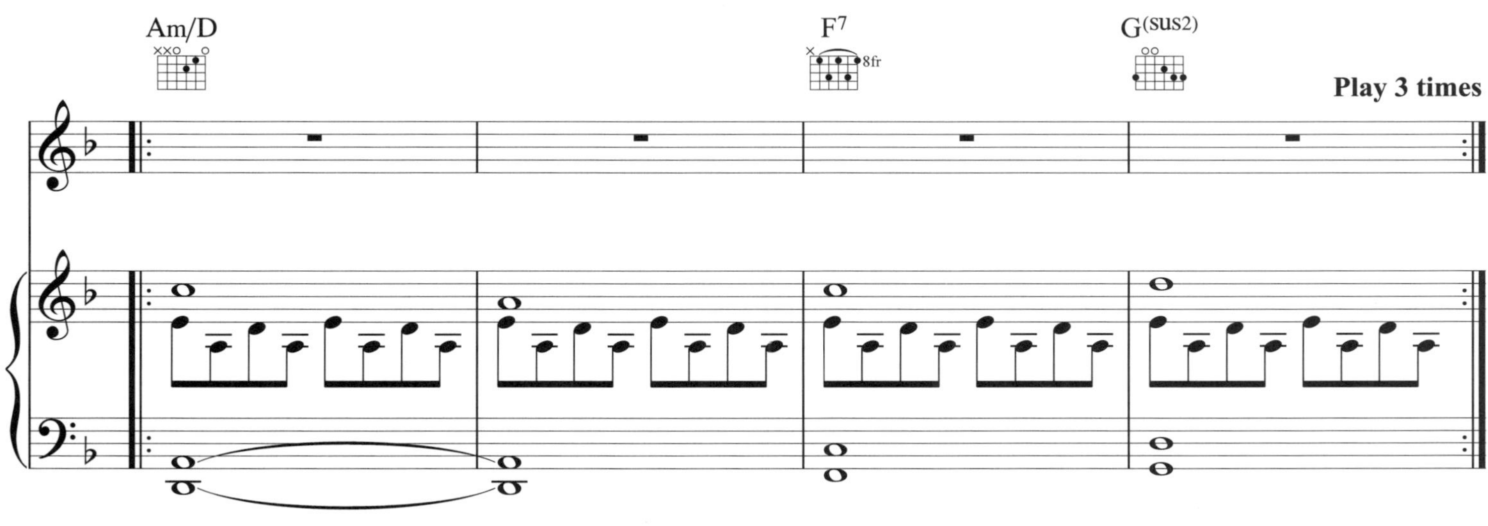
Am/D
F7
8fr
G(sus2)
Play 3 times

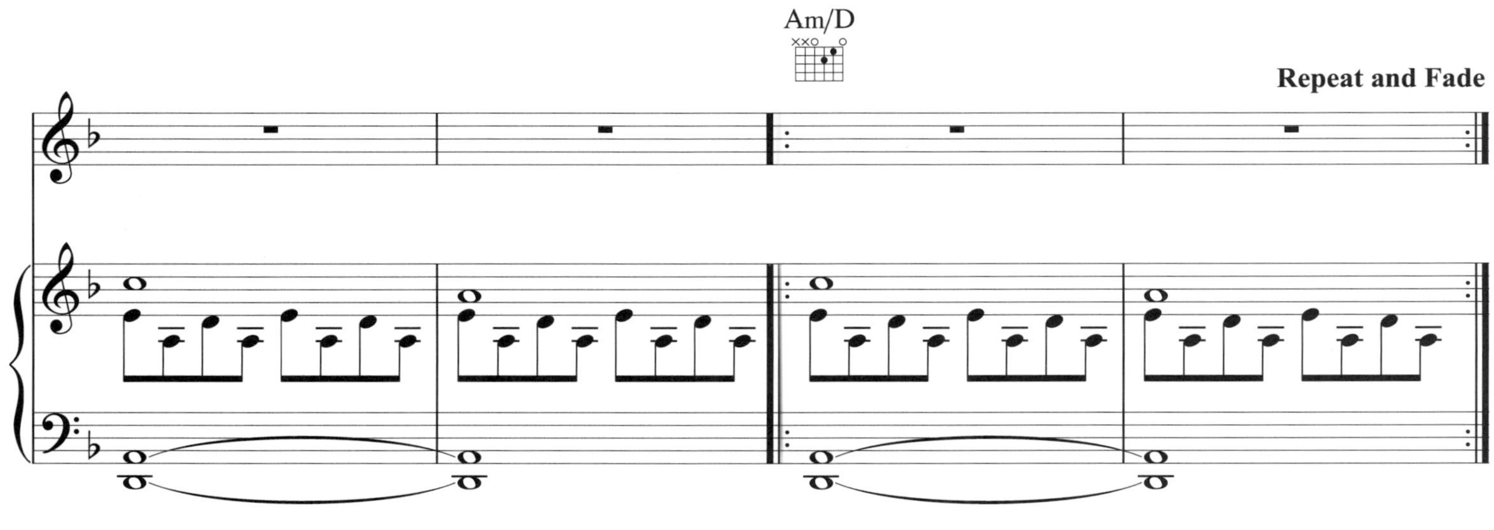
Am/D
Repeat and Fade

BOYZ II MEN

End Of The Road

Words & Music by Kenny Edmonds, Antonio Reid & Daryl Simmons

A♭
Gm7
Fm7
B♭9sus4
Why do you play with my heart? Why do you play with my mind?
You've nev - er been there be - fore, it's on - ly your first time.
E♭
E♭sus4
E♭
B♭/C
Cm
You said we'd be for - ev - er, said it'd nev - er die.
May - be I'll for - give you, may - be you'll try.
A♭
Gm7
Fm7
B♭9sus4
How could you love me and leave me and nev - er say good - bye? Well, I
We should be hap - py to - geth - er, for - ev - er, you and I. Could you
Cm
Cm/B
E♭/B♭
Am7♭5
can't sleep at night with - out hold - ing you tight. Girl, each time I try I just break down and cry.
love me a - gain like you loved me be - fore? This time I want you to love me much more.
4fr
3fr
6fr
2fr

A♭maj7
4fr
Gm7
3fr
Fm7
A♭maj7/B♭
(1.) Pain in my head, oh, I'd rath - er be dead, spin-nin' a-round and a - round.
(2. 3.) This time in-stead, just come to my bed and, ba - by just don't let me down.
Al-though we've
E♭
6fr
E♭sus4
E♭
B♭/C
Cm
come to the end of the road, still I can't let you
A♭
Gm7
Fm7
A♭maj7/B♭
go. It's un-nat-u-ral. You be-long to me, I be-long to you.
E♭
E♭sus4
E♭
B♭/C
Cm
Come to the end of the road, still I can't let you

Verse 3: (Spoken)
Girl, I'm here for you.
All those times at night when you just hurt me,
And just ran out with that other fellow,
Baby, I knew about it.
I just didn't care.
You just don't understand how much I love you, do you?
I'm here for you.
I'm not out to go out there and cheat all night just like you did, baby.
But that's alright, huh, I love you anyway.
And I'm still gonna be here for you 'til my dyin' day, baby.
Right now, I'm just in so much pain, baby.
'Cause you just won't come back to me, will you?
Just come back to me.

Yes, baby, my heart is lonely.
My heart hurts, baby, yes, I feel pain too.
Baby please...

JANET JACKSON

That's The Way Love Goes

Words & Music by Janet Jackson, James Harris III, Terry Lewis, James Brown, Charles Bobbit, Fred Wesley & John Starks

E♭maj7
6fr
F6
Gm
3fr
3
3
moth to a flame, burned_ by the fire.
My love is blind,_ can't you see my de- sire?
E♭maj7
6fr
F6
Like a moth to a flame, burned_ by the fire.
My
Gm
3fr
3
3
love is blind,_ can't you see my de- sire?
That's the_ way
E♭maj7
6fr
F6
love goes._
Like a moth to the flame, burned_ by the fire.

Gm
3fr
E♭maj7
6fr
That's the_ way love goes._ My
F6
Gm
3fr
3
3
love is blind,_ can't you see my de- sire?
E♭maj7
6fr
F6
1.Come with_ me, don't_ you wor - ry, I'm gon - na make_ you cra - zy.
3. Oh, su - gar don't_ you wor - ry, you've got_ me here_ all night.___
Gm
3fr
I'll give_ you the_ time of___ your life.___
Just close_ your eyes_ and hold_ on tight.___

E♭maj7
6fr
F6
I'm gon - na take_ you plac - es you've nev - er been_ be - fore_ and
Oh, ba - by don't_ stop, don't_ stop. Go deep - er ba - by, deep - er.
Gm
3fr
you'll be_ so hap - py that_ you came.
You feel_ so good_ I'm gon - na cry.
B♭
F/A
Dm7♭5/A♭
3
Ooh, I'm gon - na take you there. Oooh.
G7
E♭maj7
6fr
F6
That's the_ way love goes._
That's the way love

Gm
3fr
E♭maj7
6fr
goes.
That's the way love goes.
F6
To Coda
Gm
3fr
That's the way love goes.
E♭maj7
6fr
F6
2. Don't mind if I light can - dles. I like to watch us play - ing,
Gm
3fr
ba - by, I've got on what you like.

E♭maj7
6fr
F6
Come clos - er ba - by, clos - er, reach out and feel my bod - y.
Gm
3fr
D.S. al Coda
I'm gon - na give you all my love.
Coda
Gm
3fr
Gm/F
E♭maj7
6fr
goes. That's the way love goes.
F6
Gm
3fr
Gm/F
Repeat ad lib. to fade
That's the way love goes.

PORTISHEAD

Glory Box

Words & Music by Geoff Barrow, Beth Gibbons, Adrian Utley & Isaac Hayes

Cm7♭5
Bmaj7
D♯m
D♯m/C♯
6fr
to play. For I've been a temp-tress too long,
flow - ers could bloom, move o - ver and
Cm7♭5
Bmaj7
D♯m
D♯m/C♯
Cm7♭5
Bmaj7
yes. Give me a rea - son to love you.
give us some room, yeah.
D♯m
D♯m/C♯
Cm7♭5
Bmaj7
D♯m
D♯m/C♯
Give me a rea - son to be a wom - an.

1.
2.
Cm7♭5
Bmaj7
D♯m
D♯m/C♯
Cm7
B
6fr
3fr
I just so wan-na make_ a wom-an._
2. From this
Guitar

D♯m
D♯m/C♯
Cm7♭5
Bmaj7
6fr
So don't you_ stop be - ing a man._
Just take a lit - tle look_ from out -
- side___ when you can._
Sow___ a lit - tle ten - der - ness,_
no mat - ter if__ you__ cry.
Give me a rea - son___ to love_
___ you.___
Give me a rea - son___ to be___ a
3

D♯m
D♯m/C♯
Cm7♭5
Bmaj7
6fr
wom - an.
I just so wan - na be a wom - an.
'S'all
I wan - na be, is a wom - an.
N.C.
For this is the be - gin - ning of for - ev - er and ev - er.
D.S. to fade
(Repeat 1st Verse)
It's time to move o - ver.
'S'all I wan-na be, I'm so

TLC

Waterfalls

Words & Music by Marqueze Etheridge, Lisa Nicole Lopes, Rico Wade, Pat Brown & Ramon Murray

♩ = 86
N.C.
Drums
E♭maj9
B♭add9
D♭maj9
A♭
A♭/E♭
5fr
6fr
3fr
4fr
1. A lone-ly moth-er gaz-ing out of a win-dow star-ing at a son that she just can't touch.
2. Lit-tle Pre-cious has a nat-'ral ob-sess-ion for temp-ta-tion, but he just can't see.
(Verse 3 (rap) see block lyric)

E♭maj9
B♭add9
5fr
6fr
If at an-y time he's in a jam, she'll be by his side. But he does-n't
She gives him lovin' that his bod-y can't han-dle but all he can
D♭maj9
A♭/E♭
E♭maj9
B♭add9
3fr
4fr
5fr
6fr
re-al-ize he hurts her so much.
say is "ba-by it's good to me."
But all the pray-in' just ain't
One day he goes and takes a
D♭maj9
A♭add9
3fr
4fr
help-ing at all 'cause he can't seem to keep him-self out of trou - ble. So he goes out
glimpse in the mir - ror, but he does-n't re-cog-nise his own face.
E♭maj9
B♭add9
D♭maj9
A♭/E♭
5fr
6fr
3fr
4fr
and he makes his mon-ey the best way he knows how. An-oth-er bod-y lay-ing cold in the gut-
His health is fad-ing and he does-n't know why, three let-ters took him to his fi-nal rest-ing place.

To Coda ⊕
E♭maj9
5fr
B♭add9
6fr
- ter. Lis - ten to me.
Don't go chas - ing wa - ter - falls, please stick to the
D♭maj9
3fr
A♭
4fr
E♭maj9
5fr
B♭add9
6fr
riv - ers and the lakes that you're used to.
I know that you're gon - na have it your way or noth -
1.
D♭maj9
3fr
A♭/E♭
4fr
- ing at all. But I think you're mov - ing too fast.
2.
E♭maj9
5fr
B♭add9
6fr
Don't go chas - ing wa - ter - falls, please stick to the
3

D♭maj9
3fr
A♭
4fr
E♭maj9
5fr
B♭add9
6fr
riv - ers and the lakes that you're used to.
I know that you're gon - na have it your way or noth -
D♭maj9
3fr
A♭/E♭
4fr
D.S. al Coda
- ing at all.
But I think you're mov - ing too fast.
Oh, come on.
Coda
E♭maj9
5fr
B♭add9
6fr
Don't go chas - ing wa - ter - falls,
please stick to the
D♭maj9
3fr
A♭
4fr
E♭maj9
5fr
B♭add9
6fr
riv - ers and the lakes that you're used to.
I know that you're gon - na have it your way or noth -

Verse 3: (Rap)
I seen a rainbow yesterday
But too many storms have come and gone
Leaving a trace of not one God-given ray
Is it because my life is ten shades of grey?
I pray all ten fade away
Seldom praise Him for sunny days
And like His promise is true
Only my faith can undo
The many chances I blew
To bring my life to anew.
Clear blue and unconditoinal skies
Have dried the tears from my eyes, no more lonely cries
My only bleedin' hope is for the folk who can't cope
With such endurung pain
That keeps them in the pourin' rain.
Who's to blame for tootin' caine in your own vein?
What a shame.
You shoot and aim for someone else's brain
You claim the insane
And name this day in time for fallin' prey to crime
I say the system got you victim to your own mind
Dreams are hopeless aspirations
In hopes are comin' true
Believe in yourself, the rest is up to me and you.

Don't go chasing waterfalls *etc.*

The Fugees

Killing Me Softly With His Song

Words by Norman Gimbel
Music by Charles Fox

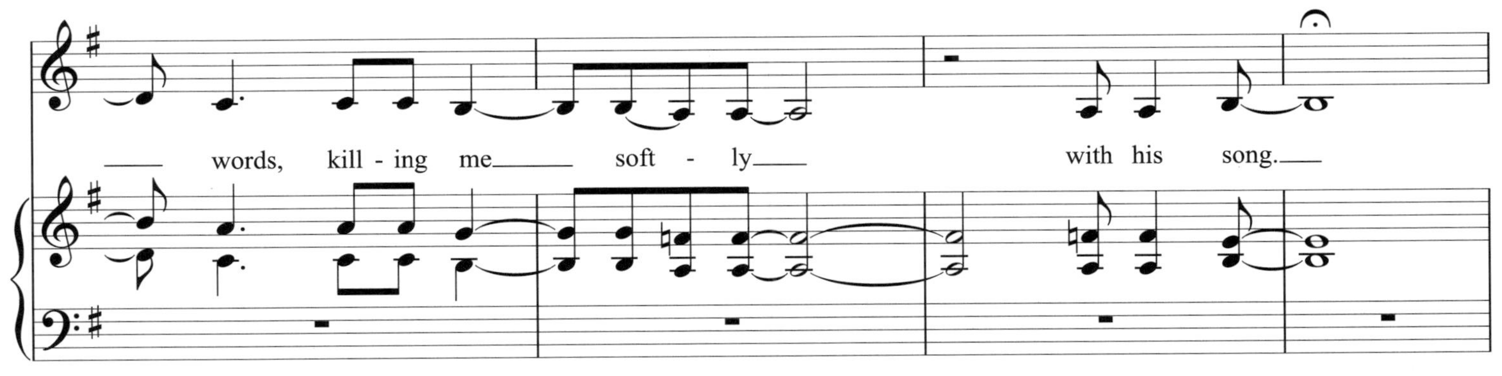
words, kill - ing me soft - ly with his song.

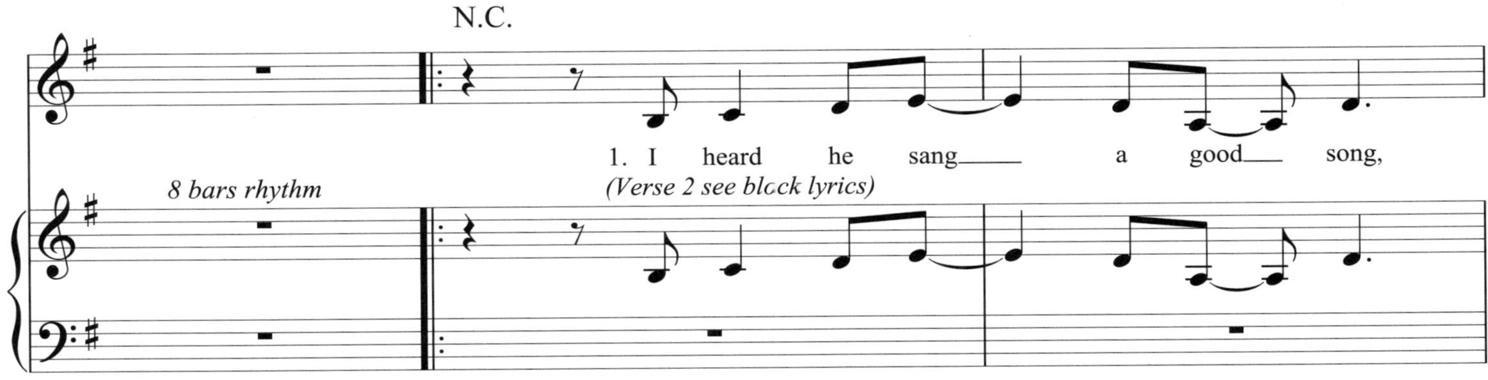
N.C.
1. I heard he sang a good song,
8 bars rhythm
(Verse 2 see block lyrics)

I heard he had a style, and so I came

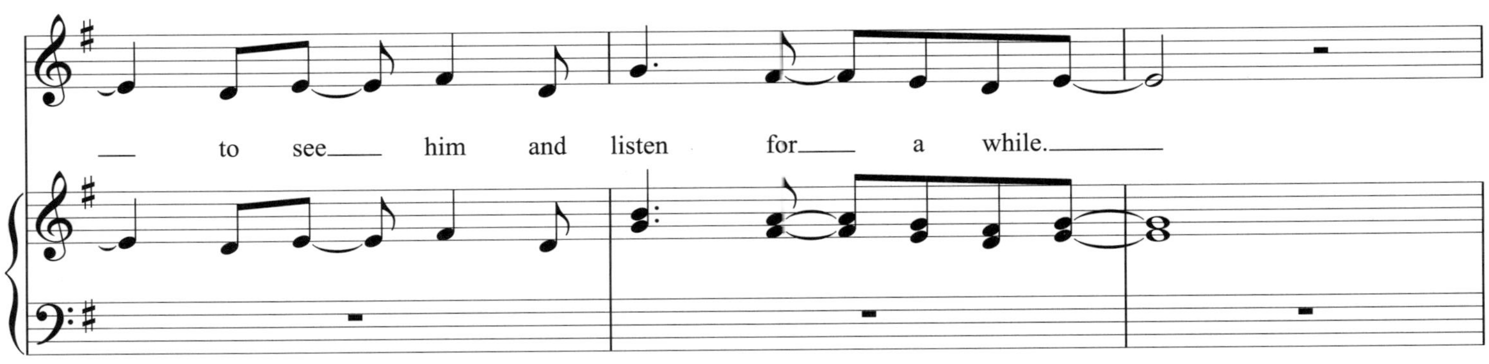
to see him and listen for a while.

and there he was, this young boy, a strang - er to my eyes.
Em
Am
D
Strum - ming my pain with his fin - gers, sing - ing my life with his words,
G
Em
A
kill - ing me soft - ly with his song, kill - ing me soft -
D
C
G
- ly with his song, tell - ing my whole life with his

C
F
words, kill - ing me soft - ly
with his song
1.
E
2.
E
Em
A
D
Oh,
oh.
G
Em
A
La la la la la la, whoa,

D
C
G
F
la.
Whoa,
la,
E
la.
Em
Am
D
Strum - ming my pain with his fin - gers,
sing - ing my life with his words,
G
Em
A
kill - ing me soft - ly with his song,
kill - ing me soft -

Verse 2:
I felt all flushed with fever,
Embarrassed by the crowd,
I felt he found my letters
And read each one out loud,
I prayed that he would finish
But he just kept right on...

ERYKAH BADU

On & On

Words & Music by Erykah Badu & Jahmal Cantero

Gmaj7/B Dmaj7/E
1. Peace and bless-ings ma-ni-fest with ev-'ry les-son learned.
(2.) man that knows some-thing knows that he knows noth-ing at all. Does it seem
(3.) rush in-to de-struc-tion 'cause you don't have noth-ing left. The
If your know-ledge were your wealth then it would be well earned.
cold-er in your Sum-mer time and hot-ter in your fall?
moth-er-ship can't save you so your ass is gon' get left.
If
we were made in his i-mage then call us by our names. Most in-tel-
-lects do not be-lieve in God but they fear us just the same. Oh,

Gmaj7/B Dmaj7/E
on and on and on and on. My ci-pher keeps mov-in' like a roll-in' stone. Ooh,
on and on and on and on. All night to the break of dawn. I go
2° All night till the vul-tures swarm.
3° You can't **** with me so just leave it a-lone.
on and on and on and on. My ci-pher keeps mov-in' like a roll-in' stone. Ooh,
To Coda I
To Coda II
on and on and on and on. God damn it, I'm-a sing my song.

N.C.
I was born un-der wa-ter with three dol-lars and six dimes. Yeah, you may laugh,
Gmaj7/B Dmaj7/E
'cause you did not do your math. Like one two three. Damn, y'all feel that? Oh.
Drums
Like one two three, the world keeps turn - ing.
Oh, what a day. what a day, what a day. 2. The
D.S. al Coda I

Coda I
N.C.
Em
Em7/D
Mad props to the God Jah born.
I'm
I'm feel-ing kind-a hun-gry
Drums
Cadd9
B
Em
Em7/D
Cadd9
B7
'cause my high is com-ing down.
Don't feed me yours
'cause your food does not en-dure.
Em
Em7/D
Cadd9
B
Em
Em7/D
I think I need a cup of tea.
The world keeps burn-ing.
Oh, what a day.
Cadd9
D.S. al Coda II
N.C.
What a day, what a day.
3. You
Coda II
Gmaj7/B Dmaj7/E
oh,
(And on and on.)

If I Could Turn Back The Hands Of Time

Words & Music by R. Kelly

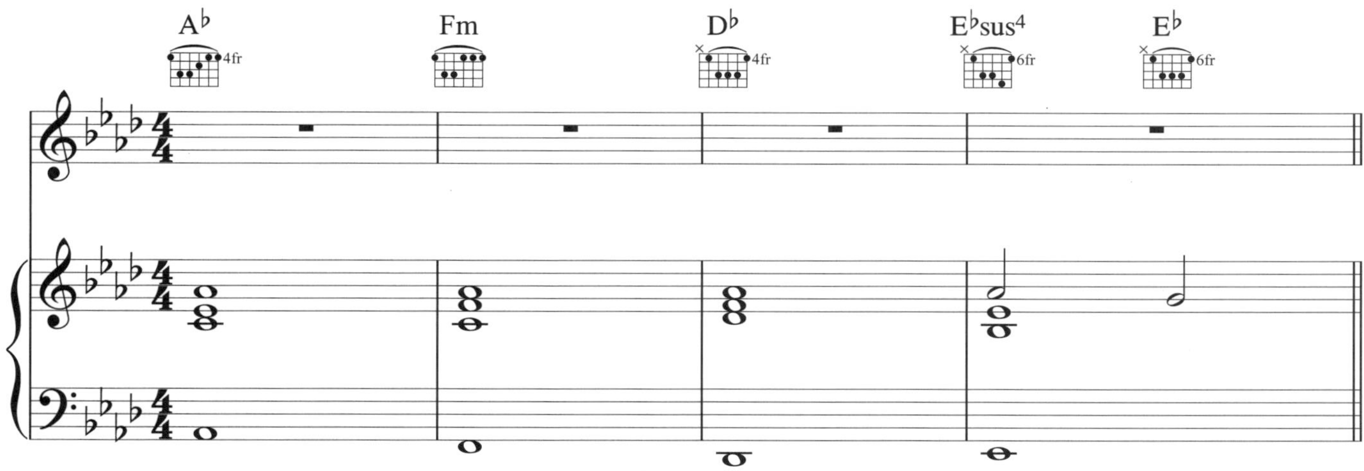
Freely, with feeling
A♭
4fr
Fm
D♭
4fr
E♭sus4
6fr
E♭
6fr

A♭
4fr
Fm
How did I ev - er let you slip a - way, nev - er

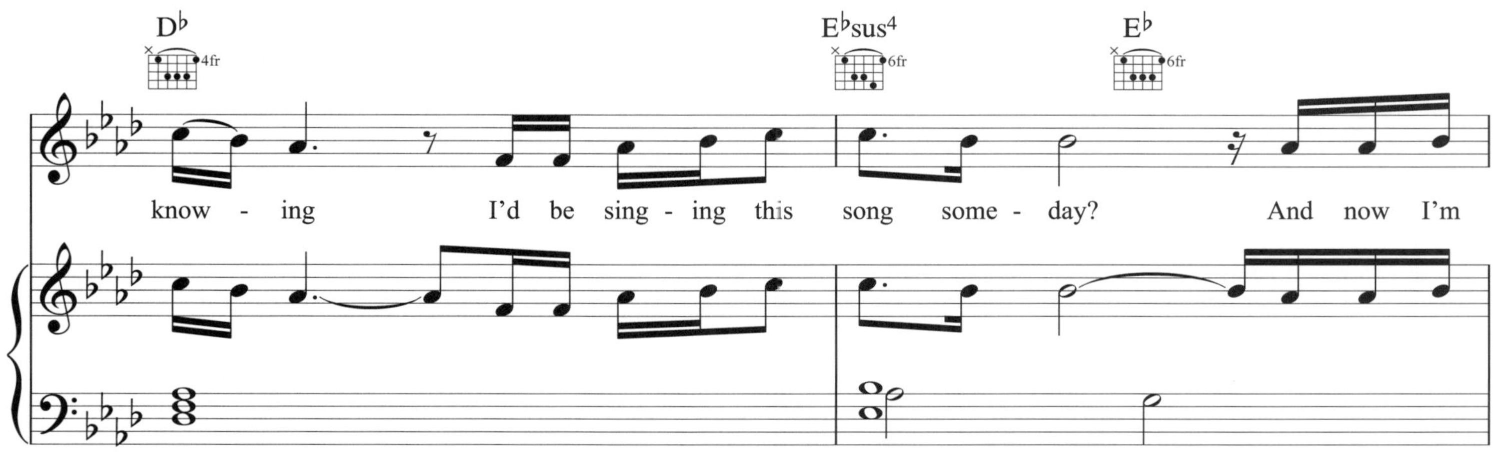
D♭
4fr
E♭sus4
6fr
E♭
6fr
know - ing I'd be sing - ing this song some - day? And now I'm

A♭
Fm
3
sink - ing, sink - ing to rise no more,
D♭
E♭sus4
E♭
ev - er since you closed the door. If I could
12/8
Smoothly ♩ = 53
A♭
Fm
turn, turn back the hands of time,
con pedale
D♭
E♭sus4
E♭
then, my dar - ling, you'd still be mine. If I

A♭
4fr
Fm
_ could turn, ___
turn
back the hands ___ of time, ___
then _
To Coda I
To Coda II
D♭
4fr
E♭sus4
6fr
E♭
6fr
dar - ling, you'd ___
you'd still be mine. ___
A♭
4fr
Fm
Fun ny, ___
fun - ny how time goes by
D♭
4fr
E♭sus4
6fr
E♭
6fr
and bless - ings ___ are missed ___
in the wink ___ of an eye. ___
Whoa, ___ why,

A♭
4fr
Fm
oh, why, oh, why should one have to go on suf-fer-ing when ev-er-
D♭
4fr
E♭sus4
6fr
E♭
6fr
-y day I plead, "Please come back to me?"
D.S. al Coda I
Coda I
E♭sus4
6fr
E♭
6fr
If I could
mine. And
D♭
4fr
E♭
6fr
Fm
you had e - nough love for the both of us but

D♭
E♭
Fm
E♭
D♭
4fr
6fr
6fr
4fr
I, I, I did you wrong. I ad - mit I did, but
B♭m
E♭
6fr
now I'm fac - ing the rest of my life a- lone.
D.S. al Coda II
Coda II
E♭sus4
E♭
6fr
6fr
Whoa, if I could
mine. Oh, I'd
A♭
4fr
Fm
nev - er hurt you, nev - er do you wrong, and nev - er
(If I could turn back.) (If I could turn back.)
(2° see block lyric)

1.
2.
D♭
E♭sus4
E♭
A♭
Fm
4fr
6fr
leave your side. Turn back the hands. Whoa, if
(If I could turn back the hands.)
hands.)
love you.
(If I could turn back.)
Repeat ad. lib. to fade
(If I could turn back.) (If I could turn back the hands.)
2°:
Whoa, if I could just turn back that little clock on the wall
Then I'd come to realise how much I love you.

I Try

Words by Macy Gray
Music by Macy Gray, Jeremy Ruzumna, Jinsoo Lim & David Wilder

G
F♯m7
— not. I play it off, but I'm dream - ing of you.—
Em7
A
And I'll keep my cool — but I'm fiend - ing.— I try to say good -
D
A
- bye and I choke, I try to walk a - way and I stum - ble. Though I try to
Em7
Em7(add11)
G
A7sus4
hide it, it's clear,— my world crum - bles when you are not here. Good -

D
A
-bye and I choke, I try to walk a - way and I stum - ble. Though I try to
Em7
G
A7sus4
1.
2.
hide it, it's clear, my world crum - bles when you are not here.
crum - bles when you are not here.
Fmaj7
Am7
Here is my con - fes - sion. May I be your pos -
Fmaj7
Em7
- ses - sion? Boy, I need your touch, your love, kiss - es and

C9
Bm7
such. With all my might I try, but this I can't de - ny,
Em7
G
de - ny. I play it off but I'm dream -
F#m7
Em7
A
B♭
- ing of you. And I'll keep my cool, but I'm fiend - ing I try to say good -
E♭
6fr
B♭
- bye and I choke, I try to walk a - way and I stum - ble. Though I try to

Verse 2:
I may appear to be free
But I'm just a prisoner of your love
And I may seem alright
And smile when you leave
But my smiles are just a front, just a front
Hey! I play it off, but I'm dreaming of you
And I'll keep my cool but I'm fiending.

I try to say goodbye and I choke *etc.*

Amy Winehouse

Joss Stone

Mary J. Blige

Duffy

KELIS

Caught Out There

Words & Music by Chad Hugo & Pharrell Williams

Gm9
3fr
1. Last year, Val - en - tine's day, you would just warm - ly say "Babe I
2. So sick of your games. I'll set your truck to flames and watch it
Cm9
A♭maj9
love you, love you babe, I swear."
blow up, blow up. Tell me (Spoken:) how you gon - na see her now?
Held you when you were sick, heav - ing. The whole
So far from sin - cere, fab - ri - ca - tions in my ear drive
time I think to my - self this is - n't fair.
me so far up the wall I come slid - ing down.

Gm9
3fr
What it this I see? (No.) You don't come home to me. (Oh,
Cm9
A♭maj9
Gm9
no.) When you don't come home to me, (Mmm.) can't deal, can't bear.
You keep tell-ing me lies, but to your sur-prise, look I
To Coda
found her red coat and you're
2° hope you're hap-py since you're
𝄋 got some-thing for you since you're
caught out there.

1° tacet
Gm9
3fr
Cm9
(Yo.) (Yo.) (Yo.) (Yo.) (Yo.)
Gm9
3fr
Cm9
(Yo.) (Yo.) (Yo.) (Yo.) (Yo.)
Gm9
3fr
3
3
I hate you so much right now. I hate you so much right now.
Cm9
A♭maj9
Gm9
3fr
3
Aah.
I hate you so much right now.
2° 3. She's so

1.
I hate you so much right now. I hate you so much right now.
Cm9
A♭maj9
Gm9
3fr
Aah.
I hate you so much right now.
2.
Gm9
3fr
(3.) raun - chy, so vul - gar. Not me, why the hell her? Look, she
Cm9
A♭maj9
Gm9
3fr
dress - es a mess, what do you see?

Gm9
3fr
It's not all a - bout cash, not how much you flash. How I
Cm9
A♭maj9
Gm9
3fr
D.S. al Coda
dress is a re - flec - tion on me.
Coda
Gm9
3fr
3
I hate you so much right now. I hate you so much right now.
Cm9
A♭maj9
1, 2.
Gm9
3fr
3.
Gm9
3fr
Aah. I hate you so much right now. I hate you so much right now.

DESTINY'S CHILD

Survivor

Words & Music by Beyoncé Knowles, Anthony Dent & Matthew Knowles

G#m
C#m7/G#
D#7/G
G#sus2
D#
4fr
3fr
6fr
broke with-out_ you, but I'm rich-er. You thought that I'd be sad with-out_you, I laugh hard-er. Thought I would-n't
grow_with-out_ you, now I'm wis-er. Thought that I'd be help-less with-out you, but I'm smart-er. You thought that I'd be
stressed with-out_ you, but I'm chill-in'. You thought I would-n't sell with-out_you, sold nine mil-lion. I'm a sur-
C#m7
D#7
-vi-vor, I'm not gon' give up. I'm not gon' stop, (What.) I'm gon' work hard-er. I'm a sur-

G#m
4fr
C#m7
4fr
D#7
6fr
G#sus2
D#
6fr
-vi - vor, I'm gon - na make it, I will sur - vive, (What.) keep on sur- vi - vin'. I'm a sur-
G#m
4fr
C#m7
4fr
D#7
6fr
G#sus2
D#
6fr
-vi - vor, I'm not gon' give up. I'm not gon' stop, (What.) I'm gon' work hard - er. I'm a sur-
1.
G#m
4fr
C#m7
4fr
To Coda
D#7
6fr
G#sus2
D#
6fr
-vi - vor, I'm gon - na make it, I will sur- vive, (What.) keep on sur- vi- vin'. 2. Thought I could-n't
2.
D#7
6fr
G#sus2
D#
6fr
G#m
4fr
C#m7/G#
4fr
-vive, (What.) keep on sur- vi - vin'. Wish - ing you the best, prais- es you are blessed

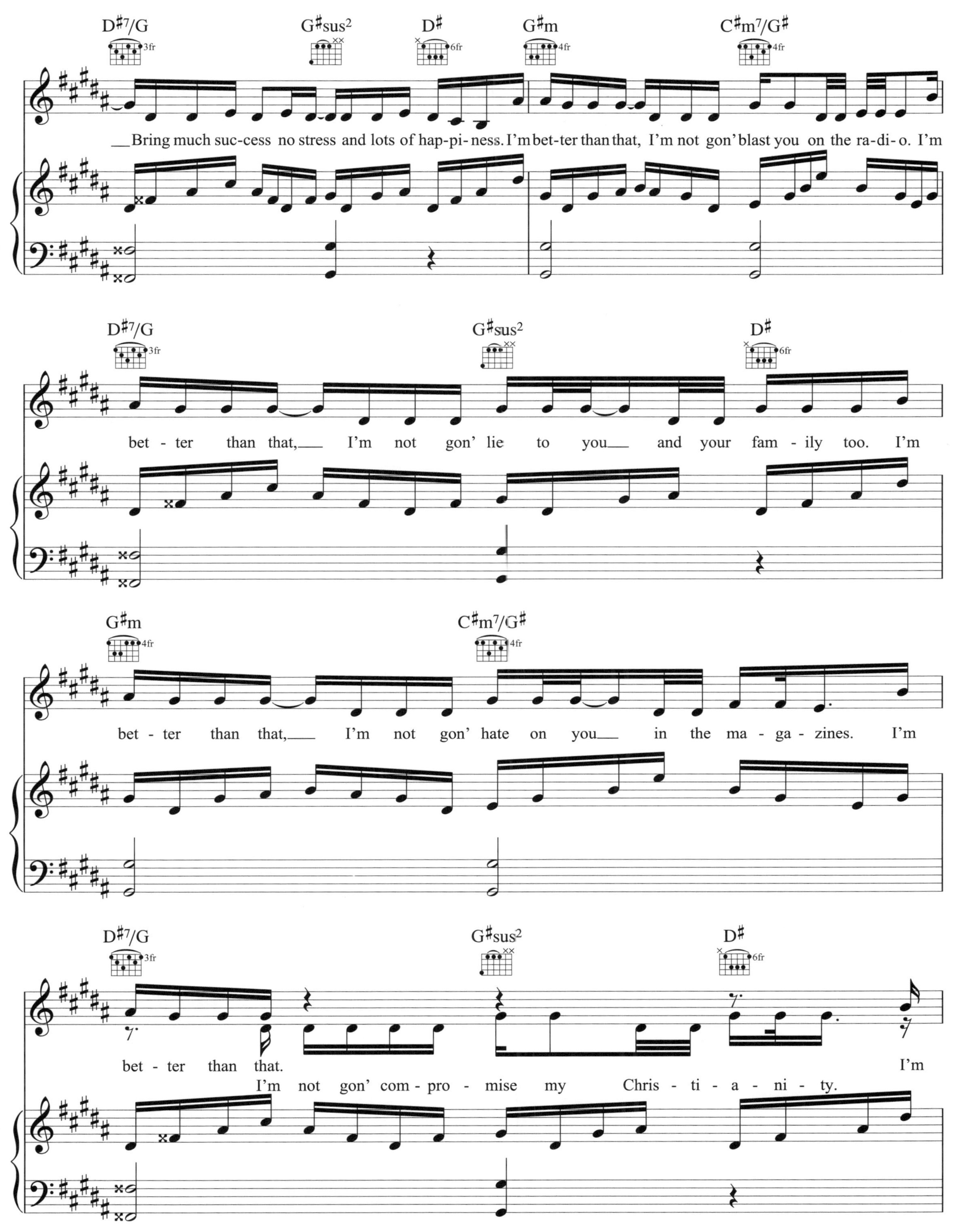
D♯7/G
G♯sus2
D♯
G♯m
C♯m7/G♯
3fr
6fr
4fr
__Bring much suc-cess no stress and lots of hap-pi-ness. I'm bet-ter than that, I'm not gon' blast you on the ra-di-o. I'm
bet - ter than that,__ I'm not gon' lie to you__ and your fam - ily too. I'm
bet - ter than that,__ I'm not gon' hate on you__ in the ma - ga - zines. I'm
bet - ter than that. I'm
I'm not gon' com - pro - mise my Chris - ti - a - ni - ty.

G#m
4fr
C#m7/G#
4fr
bet - ter than that.
You know I'm not gon' diss you on the in - ter - net,
D#7/G
3fr
G#sus2
D#
6fr
D.S. al Coda
'cause my ma - ma taught me bet - ter than that. I'm a sur -
Coda
D#7/G
3fr
G#sus2
D#
6fr
G#m
4fr
C#m7
4fr
- vive, (What.) keep on sur vi - vin'.
Oh,
oh,
D#7
6fr
G#sus2
D#
6fr
G#m
4fr
C#m7
4fr
Oh.
oh,
Oh. oh.
Oh. oh,

D♯7
G♯sus2
D♯
G♯m
C♯m7
6fr
4fr
Oh. oh, Oh. oh, oh, oh, oh, After all of the dark-ness and
sad-ness, soon comes hap-pi-ness. If I sur-round my-self with po-si-tive
things I'll gain pros-pe-ri-ty
I'm a sur-vi-vor, I'm not gon' give up. I'm not gon'
stop, (What.) I'm gon' work hard-er. I'm a sur-vi-vor, I'm gon-na make it, I will sur-

Verse 2:
Thought I couldn't breathe without you, Im inhalin'
Thought I couldn't see without you, perfect vision.
Thought I couldn't last without you, but I'm lastin'
Thought that I would die without you, but I'm livin'.
Thought that I would fail without you, but I'm on top
Thought that it would be over by now, but it won't stop.
Thought that I would self-destruct, but I'm still here
Even in my years to come, I'm still gonna be here.

I'm a survivor *etc.*

THE ROOTS FEATURING CODY CHESNUTT

The Seed (2.0)

Words & Music by Cody ChestnuTT & Tariq Trotter

♩ = 110
Am
D
Am
D
Am
Drums
1. Knocked
up nine months a - go___ and what she fit - tin'a have she don't know._ She want
(2.) - lac need space to roam._ Where we head - in' for she don't know._ We in the

D
Am
ne - o - soul,__ this hip hop is old.__ She don't want no rock and roll.__ She want
cit - y where the pros shake, rat - tle and roll. And I'm a gad - dang rol - lin' stone._ I don't
pla - ti - num, ice and gold._ She want a whole lot - ta some - thing to fold._ If you a
beg, I can hold my own._ I don't break, I can hold the chrome; and this
ob - sta - cle__ she just drop ya cold,_ 'cause one mon - key don't stop the show,_ lit - tle Mar - y is
weigh - ing a ton,_ I'm a son of a gun. My code name is The On - ly One_ and Black Thought is bad.
bad. In these streets she done ran__ ev - er since when the heat be - gan._ I told the girl "look here,
In these streets he done ran__ ev - er since when the game be - gan._ I nev - er play the fool.

D
Am
D
Am
calm down I'm - a hold your hand_ to en - a - ble you to peep the plan". _'Cause you is quick to learn_
Mat - ter fact I be keep - in' it cool since mon - ey been chan - ging hands._ And I'm left to
D
Am
D
Am
_ and we can make mon - ey to burn_ if you al - low me to lay this game._ I don't ask for
shine, the le - ga - cy I leave be - hind_ be the seed that I'll keep the flame._ I don't ask for
D
Am
D
Am
much, but e - nough room to spread my wings._ And the world fit - tin'a know my name. I don't ask_
much, but e - nough room to spread these wings._ And the world fit - tin'a know my name. I don't beg_
D
Am
D
Am
D
Am
for much these days._
from no rich man._

D
B♭
D7
And I don't bitch and whine if I don't get my way.
And I don't scream and kick when his shit don't fall in my hands,
Am
D
Am
D
Am
C
G
I only wanna fertilize another behind my lov-
man, 'cause I know how to steal. Fertilize another against my lov-
Dm
G
C
G
Dm
G
-er's back. I sit and watch it grow roots standin' where I'm at. Ferti-
-er's will. I lick the opposition 'cause she don't take no pill.
C
G
Dm
D7
-lize another behind my lov-er's back. And I'm keeping my secrets mine.
Ooh, look, dear. You'll be keeping my legend alive.

Dm7 G7 Am G Dm G
I push my seed in her bush for life. It's gon-na
Am G Dm G Fmaj7
work be-cause I'm push-in' it right. If Mar-y drops my ba-by girl to-night.
1.
Em7 B♭ Am D Am D Am
I would name her Rock-n - roll.
D Am D Am
2.
Em7 B♭
2. Ca-dil - I would name her Rock-n -

E
E7/G♯
Am
-roll. Oh, ooh, break it down, break it down, down beat.
Drums
Dm
E
Am
G
Dm
Gm
E
E/G♯
I push my
Am
G
Dm
G
Am
G
seed some-where deep in her chest. I push it na-ked 'cause I've ta-ken my test.
seed in her bush for life. It's gon-na work be-cause I'm push-ing it right.

1.
Dm
G
Fmaj7
Deliver it Mary, it don't matter the sex.
If Mary drops my
Em7
B♭
Am
D
Am
D
Am
I'm gon' name it Rock-n-roll.
I pushed my
2.
Fmaj7
Em7
B♭
Am
D
Am
3
baby girl tonight I would name her Rock-n-roll.
1-3.
D
Am
I would name her Rock-n-
4.
D
Am/G♯
Am

AMY WINEHOUSE

Help Yourself

Words & Music by Amy Winehouse, James Hogarth, Freddy James & Larry Stock

Dmaj9
C#m7
E7
I don't care, I feel the weight your shoul - ders bear.
dra - ma queen, 'cause it's where you at not where you been. So
Amaj7
Dmaj9
C#m7
Now I real - ly em - pa - thise, look - ing through your
what do you ex - pect from me? To hold your head a -
E
Amaj7
Dmaj9
blood - shot eyes. And I know you, you so frus - tra - ted.
-bove the sea? And car - ry you e - ven though you big - ger, 'cause
C#m7
F#7
Bm7
But we all be - come what we once hat - ed. Be - sides
don't you know you crush my ti - ny fig - ure? And an - y - way we're

E
Bm7
E
no-bod-y can be that wise.
still so young. Yeah, I'm still young. And this is-n't yes-ter-day.
3
Amaj7
F♯m7
Bm9
E9sus4
I can't help you if you won't help your-self.
8vb
Amaj7
F♯m7
Bm9
E13♭9
(If you won't help your-self.) (Help your-self.) No,
3
Amaj7
F♯m7
Bm9
E9sus4
Amaj7
F♯m7
I can't help you if you don't help your-self. (Help your-self.)

Bm9 E13♭9 Amaj7 F♯m7 Bm9 E9sus4
You can on-ly get so much from some-one.
Amaj7 F♯m7 Bm9 E13♭9 Amaj7 F♯m7
(Yeah.) (Oh, yeah.) I can't help you if
Bm9 E9sus4 Amaj7 F♯m7 Bm9 E13♭9
you won't help your-self.
Dmaj7 D♯dim7 A E/G♯
You might be twen-ty five but in my mind I see you as six-teen years old

F♯7
Dmaj7
D♯dim7
most the time. And I'm, I'm just a child and you full grown.
Bm9
E7
Amaj7
F♯m7
And no it's like noth-ing that I've ev-er known. Yeah, un-like
Bm9
E9sus4
Amaj7
F♯m7
Bm9
E13♭9
noth-ing that I ev-er known.
8vb
8vb
Repeat ad lib. to fade
Amaj7
F♯m7
Bm9
E9sus4
Amaj7
F♯m7
Bm9
E13♭9
Instrumental solo

JOSS STONE

Right To Be Wrong

Words & Music by Joss Stone, Desmond Child & Betty Wright

Bm11
Aadd9
I'm step-ping out into the great un - known,
Gadd9
D
Bm11
3
I'm feel-ing wings though I've nev-er flown.
Got a mind of my
Aadd9
Gadd9
own,
I'm flesh and blood
D
Bm11
3
to the bone, I'm not made of stone.
Got a right to be

Aadd9
Gadd9
N.C.
wrong, so just leave me a - lone.
D
Dsus4
D
A
Got a right to be wrong, I've been held down too
G
D
Bm
long, I've got to break free so I can fi - nal - ly breathe. Got a right to be wrong,
A
Gadd9
D
got to sing my own song, I might be sing-ing out of key but it sure feels good to

Bm
A
To Coda
Gadd9
N.C.
me. Got a right to be wrong, so just leave me a-lone.
A
G
You're en-tit-led to your o-pi-nion, but it's real-ly my de-ci-sion, I
D
Bm
can't turn back, I'm on a mis-sion, if you care don't you dare blur my vi-sion. But
A
G
let me be all that I can be, don't smo-ther me with ne-ga-ti-vi-ty,

D
Asus4
what-ev-er's out there wait - ing for me,
I'm gon-na face it will - ing - ly.
N.C.
D.S. al Coda
Mm.
Got a right to be
Coda
Gadd9
N.C.
D
so just leave me a - lone.
Mm,
Bm7
A
Gadd9
mm,
mm,

D
Bm7
A
mm,
mm,
mm,
Gadd9
D
3
mm.
Got a right, got a right,
Bm7
A
got a right, got a right.
Oh.
Gadd9
D

Be Without You

Words & Music by Mary J. Blige, Bryan Michael Cox, Johntá Austin & Jason Perry

Dm Gm9 3fr C A7
noth-ing o - ver night 'cause a love like this_ takes some time.___ Peo-ple swore it
would you lie? (No.) Make me cry? (No.) Do some - thing be-hind my back and then try to cov - er it up? Well
Dm B♭maj7 C Am7
off as a phase, said_ we can't see that. Now from top to bot-tom they_ see that we did that.
neith - er would I___ ba - by. My love is on - ly your love.
Dm Gm9 3fr C A7
(Yes.) It's so true that (Yes.) we been through it. (Yes.) We got real (sh). (Yes.) See ba - by, we been
(Yes.) I'll be faith - ful. (Yes.) I'm for real. (Yes.) And with us you'll al - ways know the deal. We've been
Dm B♭maj7 C Am7
too strong for too long. (And I can't be with - out___ you ba - by.) And I'll be wait - ing

Dm
Gm9
3fr
C
A7
up un-til you get home. ('Cause I can't sleep with out__ you ba - by.) An-y-bod-y
Dm
B♭maj7
C
Am7
who's ev - er loved, ya know_ just what I feel. Too hard to fake it, noth-ing can re-place it.
Dm
Gm9
3fr
To Coda
C
A7
Call the ra-di-o if you_ just can't be with-out__ your ba - by.
Gm7
3fr
Am7
B♭maj7
Am7
See this is real__ talk, I'm-a al-ways stay.__ (No mat-ter what.) Good or

Gm7
3fr
Am7
B♭maj7
A7
3
bad. (Thick and thin.) Right or wrong. (All day, ev-'ry day.) Now if you're
Dm
N.C.
down on love or don't be - lieve, this ain't for you. (No, this ain't for you.)
And if you get it
Drums
3
deep in your heart and deep down you know that it's true, well, let me see you put your
Dm7
B♭maj7
C
Am7
hands up. (Fel - las tell your la - dy she's the one.) Oh, put your

Dm7
B♭maj7
C
A7
D.S. al Coda
hands up. (La-dies let him know he got your love.)
Look him right in his eyes and tell him we been
Coda
C
A7
your ba - by. Hey!
Dm
B♭maj7
C
Am7
Oh.
Dm
Gm9
3fr
3
C
A7
Repeat ad lib. to fade
Oh.
Hey!

Crazy

Words & Music by Thomas Callaway, Brian Burton, Gianfranco Reverberi & Gian Piero Reverberi

A♭
Gsus4
G
e - cho in so much space.
Cm
And when you're out there, with - out care, yeah, I was out of touch.
2. Come on now, who do you, who do you, who do you, who do you think you
E♭maj7
A♭add9
But it was-n't be - cause I did-n't know e - nough.
are? Ha, ha, ha, bless your soul.
A♭
Gsus4
G
I just knew too much.
Does that make me cra -
You real - ly think you're in con - trol.
Well, I think you're cra -

Cm
3fr
E♭maj7
6fr
- zy? Does that make me cra - zy?
- zy. I think you're cra - zy.
- zy. May - be you're cra - zy.
A♭add9
4fr
A♭
4fr
Does that make me cra - zy? Pos - sib - ly.
I think you're cra - zy, just like me.
May - be we're cra - zy. Prob - ab - ly.
Gsus4
G
To Coda
C
And I hope that you are hav - ing the time of your
My he - roes had the heart to lose their lives out on a limb.

A♭add9
4fr
A♭
4fr
E♭maj7
6fr
life.
But think twice,
And all I re - mem - ber is
Gsus4
G
that's my on - ly ad - vice.
think - in' I wan - na be like them.
Cm
3fr
3. Ev - er since I was lit - tle, ev - er since I was lit - tle it looked like fun.
E♭maj7
6fr
A♭add9
4fr
And it's no co - in - ci - dence I've come

A♭
4fr
Gsus4
G
D.S. al Coda
and I can die when I'm done.
But may - be I'm cra -
Coda
C
A♭add9
4fr
Mm.
Ooh.
A
E♭maj7
6fr
Ooh.
Ooh.
Ooh.
Gsus4
G
C
Ooh.
Ooh.
Mm.

ALICIA KEYS

No One

Words & Music by Alicia Keys, George Harry & Kerry Brothers, Jr.

E
B
C♯m
4fr
3
You can be sure that it will
you will al-ways be a-round; this I
A
E
B
on-ly get bet-ter.
know for cer-tain.
You and me to-geth-er through the days and nights.
C♯m
4fr
A
E
I don't wor-ry 'cause ev-'ry-thing's gon-na be al-right.
Peo-ple keep talk-ing,
B
C♯m
4fr
A
they can say what they like.
But all I know is ev-'ry-thing's gon-na be al-right.
*

E
B
C♯m
4fr
And no one, no one, no one can get in the way
A
E
B
of what I'm feel - ing. No one, no one, no one
C♯m
A
To Coda
can get in the way of what I feel for you.
E
B
C♯m
You, you, can get in the way

1.
A
E
of what I feel for you.
2. When the rain is pour - ing
2.
A
F♯m
B
of what I feel.
I know
some peo - ple
E/G♯
A
C♯m7
4fr
Amaj7
search the world to find
some - thing like what we have.
I
F♯m
B
E/G♯
know
peo - ple will try,
try to div - ide
some - thing so

Amaj7
E/B
B
real. So till the end of time I'm tell - ing you there ain't no
E
D.S. al Coda
Coda
E
one, no
Oh oh oh oh
B
C♯m
4fr
oh. Oh oh oh oh oh. Oh oh oh oh
Vocal tacet 3° & 4°
1, 2.
3.
A
E
E
Repeat ad lib.
oh oh oh oh oh. Oh oh oh oh

Mercy

Words & Music by Duffy & Stephen Booker

C9/D
C9
Gm
C
G7
3fr
1. I love
Gm7
you, but I got to stay true.
(2.) will be some-thing on the side
My mor-als got me on my knees, I'm beg-ging you, please, stop play-ing games.
but you've got to un-der-stand that I need a man who can take my hand.
Yes I do!
I don't know what this is but you've got me good,
C9/D

C9
Gm
3fr
just like you knew you would.
C9/D
C9
I don't know what you do but you do it well, I'm un - der your spell.
G7
3fr
You've got me beg - ging you for
G
C/G
Gm7
C/G
G
C/G
Gm7
mer - cy. Why won't you re - lease me?

C/G
Gm/C
C
Gm7/C
You got me beg - ging you for mer - - cy.
C
G
C/G
Gm7
Why won't you re - lease me?
I said re - lease
C6/9/D
C11
G
me.
1.
2.
C/G
Gm7
C/G
2. Now you think that I

N.C.
I'm beg-ging you for mer - cy, just why won't you re - lease
me?
I'm beg-ging you for mer - cy.
You got me beg - ging,
You got me beg - ging,
You got me beg - ging.
G
C/G
Gm7
C/G
G
C/G
Gm7
3fr
1. Mer - cy.
Why won't you re - lease me?
(2.) mer - cy.
I'm beg - ging you for mer - cy.

C/G Gm/C C Gm7/C C G
3fr
I'm beg - ging you for mer - cy. Why won't_ you re - lease_
I'm beg - ging you for mer - cy. I'm beg - ging you for
C/G Gm7 C6/9/D C11 G
5fr
_ me? You've got me beg-ging you for mer - - - - - cy.___
mer- cy. Why won't you re - lease_ me?___
1. 2.
C/G Gm7 C/G C/G
Yeah.___ 2. I'm beg - ging you for ___ Break it down!
Yeah.___
G7
Repeat ad lib. and fade
You got me beg- ging, beg-ging you for mer - cy. You got me beg- ging down on my knees. I said...

Happy

Words & Music by Leona Lewis, Ryan Tedder & Evan Bogart

Em
G
Dm
C
love in vain__ 'cause love won't set you free.__ I could stand by__the side
dif - f'rent fac - es, dif - f'rent names. Get me out - ta here.__ Well, I can't stand by__the side__
8vb
1° only
G
Dm
C
G
and watch this life pass__ me by.
F
Fm
So un-hap-py but safe__ as could__ be.__ So what if it
8vb
2° only
Dm
C
G
and watch__ this life pass__ me by.__ Pass__ me by.__

C
So what if it hurts me?
So what if I
Am
break down?
So what if this world just throws me off the edge, my
Fmaj7
8vb
G
C
Am
feet run out-ta ground? I got-ta find my place.
I wan-na hear my sound.
Don't care a-bout
(8)
Fmaj7
1.
G
N.C.
all the pain in front of me
'cause I'm just try-in'-a be hap-py.
8vb

C
Am
Em
3
Yeah.
Just wan-na be
hap - py.
G
2.
G
Dm
Am
Yeah.
I'm just try-in'-a be
hap-py.
C
G
Dm
Am
C
G
Hap - py.
So man-y
Dm
Am
C
G
turns that I can't see,
like I'm a stran - ger on this road.
But don't say

rit.
F
Fm
vic - tim. Don't say an - y - thing. So what if it
8vb
a tempo
C
Am
hurts me? So what if I break down? So what if this
Fmaj7
G7
N.C.
world just throws me off the edge, my feet run out - ta ground? I got - ta find
8vb
C
Am
my place. I wan - na hear my sound. Don't care a - bout

Fmaj7
G
all the pain in front of me.
I just wan - na be hap - py.
8vb
C
Am
Fmaj7
Happ - py.
Hap - py.
8vb
G
N.C.
C
I just wan - na be hap - py.
Oh.
(8)
Am
Em
G
3
Hap - py.

2 3 4 5 6 7 8 9

Bringing you the words and the music

All the latest music in print... rock & pop plus jazz, blues, country, classical and the best in West End show scores.

- Books to match your favourite CDs.
- Book-and-CD titles with high quality backing tracks for you to play along to. Now you can play guitar or piano with your favourite artist... or simply sing along!
- Audition songbooks with CD backing tracks for both male and female singers for all those with stars in their eyes.
- Can't read music? No problem, you can still play all the hits with our wide range of chord songbooks.
- Check out our range of instrumental tutorial titles, taking you from novice to expert in no time at all!
- Musical show scores include *The Phantom Of The Opera*, *Les Misérables*, *Mamma Mia* and many more hit productions.
- DVD master classes featuring the techniques of top artists.

Visit your local music shop or, in case of difficulty, contact the Marketing Department, Music Sales Limited, Newmarket Road, Bury St Edmunds, Suffolk, IP33 3YB, UK
marketing@musicsales.co.uk